Contents

List of Tables and Figures

CONFINTEA VI
United Kingdom National Report

Report on the
ment and State
t of Adult Learning
cation (ALE)

United Kingdom
National Commission for UNESCO

promoting adult learning

Department for
**Innovation,
Universities &
Skills**

Published by the National Institute of Adult Continuing Education
(England and Wales)

21 De Montfort Street
Leicester LE1 7GE
Company registration no. 2603322
Charity registration no. 1002775

NIACE, the national organisation for adult learning, has a broad remit to promote
lifelong learning opportunities for adults. NIACE works to develop increased
participation in education and training, particularly for those who do not have easy
access because of barriers of class, gender, age, race, language and culture, learning
difficulties and disabilities, or insufficient financial resources.

NIACE's website on the Internet is http://www.niace.org.uk

Cataloguing in Publication Data
A CIP record of this title is available from the British Library

ISBN 978 1 86201 381 0

Typeset and designed by Boldface, London
Printed by Latimer Trend, Plymouth

Acknowledgements

This report has been written for the UK Government by Stephen McNair and Lucia Quintero-Re, with additional material from Alan Clarke, Jan Eldred, Anita Hallam, Peter Lavender, Joan O'Hagan, Richard Pearce, Alastair Thomson, Alan Tuckett, and Kate Watters. (all are staff of the National Institute of Adult Continuing Education (NIACE), and from Mike Osborne and John Tibbett of the PASCAL Observatory at Glasgow University, and Lynn Tett of Edinburgh University.

NIACE is grateful for the financial assistance of the UNESCO UK Education Committee in the preparation of this report

Note on expenditure figures

All expenditure figures are stated in £ sterling. At the time of writing £1 represented approximately $2US, and €1.25

Ministerial foreword

Over the last decade, the United Kingdom has experienced a tremendous amount of social, economic, technological and cultural change – all of which have had a major influence on the role and the nature of adult learning. At the same time, this government has led the longest period of continuous economic growth on record. This has enabled us to massively increase our investment in adult education and ensure that more people have been able to reap the benefit of this. But we have also sought to make taxpayers' money work harder – reforming the way in which learning and skills have been delivered – by introducing some of the most dramatic and far-reaching changes to the education and skills system that this country has ever known.

We have seen a huge expansion of funding for adult learning - with a much greater focus on giving people the skills they need to succeed in work and in life. We have handed over more control to individuals and employers – giving them the power to determine where and when their learning takes place. And we have made tough choices about who pays for learning – introducing a much greater focus on getting those individuals and employers who can afford it, to contribute towards the cost of their learning. In doing so, I truly believe that we have transformed the way in which individuals, employers and local communities are able to access the opportunities that learning provides – helping more people to unlock their talents and realise their full potential.

These changes have been set against a backdrop of considerable social and economic change. Over the last ten years we have continued to see a rise in the overall population – but one which is increasingly characterised by its diversity and mobility. We have seen the emergence of international terrorism and the continued exclusion of some sections of society. And we have seen a real decline in absolute poverty – although we know that too many people still experience disadvantage. This has presented us with particular issues: as educationalists, and as citizens and community leaders – challenging us to do more to use the acquisition of learning and skills as a means of fostering shared values and building strong and cohesive communities. In recent years we have seen the emergence of a much greater recognition of global trends impacting on national economies. We are much more aware of the way in which our economic and social prosperity is predicated on our ability to compete successfully and globally. And we know that for the UK, this means competing on the basis of our knowledge and skills.

This government has understood the nature and impact of these intertwining social and economic trends. They have provided the context for our long-term strategy: to invest in the skills that we need now, and in the future, to maintain our position as a strong and prosperous world-class economy. Over the last ten years we have successively set out our ambition for adult skills, maintaining a clear focus on the key outcomes we have wanted to achieve: to strengthen economic competitiveness and address social exclusion by raising levels of skill and qualification. And, in order to deliver these, we have taken bold steps to devolve more and more power to the front-line – where the expertise in dealing with employers and individuals lies – and in handing more purchasing power to our customers. This has meant a radical transformation of the way in which adult skills has been delivered.

As this report clearly demonstrates: this has therefore been a decade of change – with four Acts of Parliament for education and skills and two in progress at the time of writing. But I make no apologies for this – instead I would point to all that this change has achieved:

- We have seen more young people than ever before engage in post-compulsory learning. At the end of 2007 the proportion of 16–18 year olds in education and training was 78.7 per cent, the highest rate ever.
- We have seen all learners achieving more – with success rates across the FE system increasing year on year. The overall success rate for LSC-funded learning in FE was 77 per cent in 2006/07, up from 74 per cent in 2004/05.
- We have seen the quality of provision increase massively as, simultaneously, we have delivered more intensive programmes to address economic and social needs.
- We have ensured that all adults have an entitlement to basic literacy, numeracy and first full Level 2 courses – where government investment has ensured these courses will be free for all those who are eligible.
- We have extended this entitlement to give all 19–25 year olds access to first full Level 3 courses – helping them to get the skills they need for success.
- We have seen more people than ever before go on to Higher Education, with the Higher Education Initial Participation Rate at 42 per cent in 2005/06, up by 3 percentage points from 1999/00.
- We have expanded the choice and diversity of learning on offer – for example, more people than ever are participating in a greater range of Apprenticeships.
- We have worked in genuine partnerships with employers – listening to, and acting on, their concerns – giving them a crucial role at the heart of designing and delivering the skills and qualifications their business needs.
- We have introduced an impartial service for employers – Train to Gain – which has helped thousands of businesses identify and source the training they need.
- We have seen overall levels of public funding in adult skills increase massively. Over the decade from 1995–96 to 2005–06 total expenditure by the education departments on post-compulsory education and training increased in real terms by 29 per cent to a total of £19.5 billion.
- We have delivered more for the public purse – introducing significant efficiencies whilst delivering more for individuals and employers.
- We have imported the best principles from the private sector – giving employers and individuals the right to make their own decisions about their learning routes and providers.
- We have promoted the value and benefits of learning – so that those who are able to pay

are prepared to invest their own time and money in getting the skills they need to succeed.

■ We are progressively getting more and more people off benefit and out of the poverty trap – by giving them the skills to get into and progress within sustainable employment.

■ We have invested more in higher level skills and higher education – to support a highly skilled, knowledge based economy.

■ We have overseen a major expansion of research into adult learning, through the Independent Research Councils, and through specialised Research Centres funded by Government

We have achieved much, but we are not complacent. We recognise that there is more we need to do if we are to unlock the talents of all individuals and enable them to progress in work and life. This report sets out some important challenges for government and the wider learning and skills system to address. As we respond to these, I believe that we are greatly helped by the particular focus that the Department for Innovation, Universities and Skills (DIUS) brings. Since 2007 and, for the first time ever, we have a Government Department that deals exclusively with post-school education and training.

The creation of DIUS recognises the interrelationship between three policy areas that are critical to determining Britain's future economic and social wellbeing. Britain can only succeed in a changing world if we develop our skills to the fullest possible extent, carry out world-class research, and apply knowledge to create innovative products, services and companies. As we experience the continued impact of global economic and social change we need now, more than ever, a continued investment in adult skills to deliver even greater social and economic success.

Bill Rammell MP
Minister of State, Lifelong Learning,
Further and Higher Education

Executive summary
the UK 1997–2008

In the decade since CONFINTEA V[1] the UK has experienced significant economic, constitutional, and social change, which has had a major influence on both the need for and nature of adult learning. Major Government powers have been devolved to elected bodies in Scotland, Wales and Northern Ireland, which have all adopted distinctive approaches to some aspects of education policy.

The population of 60 million continues to grow (except in Scotland) but mainly through extending life expectancy, and fertility rates are below replacement rate. Within the UK there is a continuing movement of population, and especially of the highly educated, to London and the South East of England. Some 12 per cent of the UK population is non-white (mainly British born), concentrated in the cities, but increasingly dispersed more widely. The population, and especially the workforce, has been significantly enlarged by a large wave of immigration from Eastern Europe, following the expansion of the European Community in 2004.

On the social front, economic growth and liberalisation has seen a widening of income gaps, and a slowing of the broad social mobility which characterised the previous decades. While absolute poverty levels have declined, especially among children and old people, social exclusion remains a policy concern.

Since the mid 1990s, the longest period of continuous economic growth on record has enabled Government to make major increases in expenditure on education and health, and on overcoming social exclusion. This growth has included expansion in funds for the education of adults, although a larger proportion has been spent on pre-school and school age children, reflecting research evidence of the long term social and economic impact of such investment.

Community cohesion and education for citizenship have become a major focus of Government policy, fed particularly by concerns about international terrorism and the social exclusion of some ethnic and religious minority groups. There has also been a focus on reducing discrimination, with established legislation outlawing discrimination on grounds of gender, race and disability extended to include age, religion and sexual orientation, and a new overarching Council for Equality and Human Rights has been created to oversee implementation, and support enforcement.

1 CONFINTEA V was the fifth International Conference on Adult Education, held in Hamburg, Germany on the 14–18 of July 1997. It is category II UNESCO conference hosted every 12 years.

Government structures

A major change has been the creation of a more centralised, and long term, process for policy development and monitoring across the UK Government. The previous system of annual budgeting has been replaced by a three yearly "Comprehensive Spending Review" where Government reviews all Government programmes, and reallocates resources. These plans are then converted into "Public Service Agreements" (30 in the current cycle) which all Departments are expected to contribute to, with specified performance indicators for each, and detailed monitoring and annual review by the Treasury. Three of the current 30 PSAs are the responsibility of the Department responsible for post-school education, but twelve have implications for adult learning.

The focus of Government policy

The decade has seen continuous change on many fronts, including in post-school education and training. By international standards, and by comparison with previous periods of UK history, there has been an unprecedented number of policy initiatives and structural changes, with four Acts of Parliament and two further ones in Parliament at the time of writing, as well as many consultative and analytical reports. The underlying direction of policy (in education as in other areas, and especially in England) has been towards, improving quality and increasing individual choice, through a more market like model of services, in which individuals and employers are enabled to make their own decisions about their learning routes and choices, and buy suitable provision from a range of quality assured providers.

Government policy has been driven by two interlinked objectives: to strengthen economic competitiveness through raising levels of skill and qualification, and to address social exclusion. The Government's view, that the most effective way of overcoming exclusion is to raise levels of employment, led in the 1990s to a strong "work first" strategy for reducing unemployment, but growing concern about low skills and sustainable employment has created a stronger focus on training and skills.

Government has sought to increase the volume of education available to adults despite the limits of public expenditure, by increasing the financial contribution made by individuals and employers, concentrating public expenditure on two priorities: those with very low skills, who need to be brought into the productive economy, and higher education, to support a highly skilled, knowledge based economy. In parallel, employers are being encouraged to increase their investment, and tuition fees have been introduced for higher education students for the first time.

In order to improve the efficiency of the "market" in education and training two new structures are being put in place to improve information and advice for employers and individuals. A brokerage service, "Train to Gain", has recently been created to assist employers to identify and source appropriate training to meet their particular business needs (and to subsidise such training when it meets broader Government priorities). Alongside this, plans are in hand for a much enhanced Adult Advancement and Careers Service, to provide information advice and support to individuals seeking appropriate education and training to meet their needs in work and in life more generally. In Scotland a new body, Skills Development Scotland, has been created with similar purposes. Furthermore, Government intends to develop an expanded system of Learner Accounts, to enable individuals to purchase courses to meet their own needs.

In relation to training for the current workforce, Government remains committed to a voluntary approach, with state intervention focused strongly on stimulating employer and individual demand by improving quality and the responsiveness of providers, and by developing supporting services to make training attractive to employers (including the creation of employer led Sector Skills Councils, a reformed qualifications system due to be rolled out from 2008, and the *Train to Gain* service). However, as the 2006 Government commissioned report on Skills pointed out, the current poor qualification base is a result of this model, and Government has indicated that it will consider regulation at a future date if employers do not voluntarily increase their investment in training.

Educational structures

There is no distinct "adult learning sector" in the UK. Adult students participate in programmes in institutions of all sectors, including Further and Higher Education, Schools, Work Based Learning Programmes, Voluntary and Community Organisations, and Local Authority Adult Education Services. Only the last of these is exclusively committed to adults, and it represents a very small proportion of the funding, although it represents a significant proportion of overall student numbers.[2] The bulk of adult learning is provided through the FE and HE institutions. However, in England 2007 saw the creation, for the first time, of a Government Department exclusively concerned with post-school education ad training (the Department for Innovation, Universities and Skills – DIUS). The new Department was created by Gordon Brown as one of this first acts as Prime Ministers to bring together three closely-linked strands of policy key to determining Britain's future: skills, innovation and research.

Most of the management of public funding for adult learning is devolved to national Funding Councils, although the pattern varies between the four countries: in Wales, Further Education is managed directly by Government, and both Further and Higher Education are managed in this way in Northern Ireland. Funding has increasingly been used to as a policy lever to intervene in the organisation and delivery of education for adults.

Key features of the decade in adult learning

Key features of education since 1997 have included:

■ A rise in total participation in the late 1990s, followed by a fall in total numbers as a result of stronger concentration on more intensive programmes targeted more directly at particular economic and social needs;

---

2 Most such students are enrolled on courses involving attendance for only 2 hours a week, usually for less than 20 weeks. As a result, their number are large, but they account for a small part of the budget.

- Progress towards the creation of an inclusive National Qualifications Framework, with three closely related frameworks in England, Scotland and Northern Ireland, embracing qualifications form the most basic literacy to Doctoral level;
- The introduction of more formal qualification requirements for teachers in all phases of post-school education;
- A major expansion of research into adult learning, especially through the Independent Research Councils, and through specialised Research Centres funded by Government
- Major improvements in the quality and quantity of routine data collection about adult learners in all sectors and phases.
- A major expansion of funding for basic education (known as Skills for Life), on which Government has spent £3.5 billion since 2000;
- Very rigorous national quality assurance systems during the early years, aimed to make major improvements in quality. As institutions have demonstrated their capability to manage quality, responsibility for this is now being progressively devolved.
- Greater focus on employers as key partners in the design and delivery of learning.

Commentary

A number of policy issues emerge from the UK experience in the last decade:

- **The impact of policy change.** There is concern that whilst Government's interventions have improved the performance of the system they have also resulted in a significant pace of change. DIUS recognises the potential impact of this and has an explicit risk management process in place to mitigate against potential adverse impact.
- **The shift to a demand-led system.** Managing the move from a centrally managed to a market model of education involves the need to work closely with the FE sector to take full advantage of the opportunities this affords and ensure a smooth shift to new models of engaging with employer and individuals that will not destabilise the supply of education during the transition.
- **The academic-vocational divide.** There is a continuing, and long running cultural problem that vocational qualifications are widely perceived as inferior to academic ones. Efforts to address this are being made through a reinvigoration of apprenticeships, and the creation of a new system of national Diplomas, embracing academic and vocational elements.
- **The unintended effects of quality assurance systems.** The concern to improve the quality of education for adults, especially for those with the lowest levels of qualification, led to the creation of rigorous but complex quality assurance systems, which made heavy demands on the time and resources of institutions and staff. These regimes are now moving towards a "light touch" approach, in the light of evidence of improved quality in most institutions.
- **The "articulation" of the education and training system.** The current range of post-school institutions is the result of a number of complex factors, with four different kinds of institution offering provision for 16–19 year olds in some areas. Mobility between the stages (at 11, 16, and 18) and between institutions of FE and HE can be difficult and present a barrier to progression for the less motivated. The issue of articulation is being addressed

on several fronts, including "widening participation" initiatives to support transitions, and by moves to create a new Qualifications and Credit Framework for England, Wales and Northern Ireland, embracing academic and vocational elements.

■ **The role and future of non-vocational education for adults.** The UK has traditionally had a very extensive range of part-time "non-vocational", non-qualification bearing adult education delivered by public and voluntary agencies at local level. This work expanded rapidly in the late 1990s, driven by a policy to use such programmes to widen participation in education generally. However, since 2004 learner numbers in this specific kind of publicly funded provision have declined significantly. This follows the new policy focus on skills and by the transition from a managed to a market led model of education for adults, which has produced rapid fee increases for many learners. Government has now launched the first major public consultation on how such provision might be best supported in the future, using the resources of public, private and voluntary sectors. The associated mapping study of the consultation also looks at whether more provision is being delivered by private and voluntary organisations using new technologies rather than more traditional classroom based models.

■ **The fluidity of ALE across institutional boundaries.** Adult learning takes place in many locations, and is organised by many agencies. Much of this is difficult to track and measure, but especially so when it moves from formal educational institutions into the voluntary sector or into other areas of public funding. It is difficult to assess how far activities formerly funded through public sector non-formal education have moved to private programmes, voluntary or self help groups or migrated into Local Authority Leisure, Library or Museum services. Although the sector's diversity is one of its greatest strengths it also makes it difficult to track the activity, and to evaluate how far the quality and accessibility of the resulting provision is comparable. The advent of new media/technologies means that learning is increasingly being delivered in new creative and innovative ways which could be impossible to measure.

■ **Qualifications and skills.** Following the Leitch report on Skills commissioned by Government and published in 2006, there has been a very strong policy focus on formal vocational qualifications. However the relationship between qualifications and the true nature and quality of skills is a hugely disputed area. Presently unpublished Government research indicates a more positive relationship between qualifications and earnings than that presented by prior research, specifically with regards to the relation between the average earnings return for NVQ2 qualifications acquired at age 26–34.

Expectations of CONFINTEA VI

The UK has made significant progress on the Hamburg Declaration's proposals in relation to:

■ Women's integration and empowerment;
■ Diversity and equality;
■ Transformation of the economy;
■ Access to information.

Progress has been more modest on:

■ Culture of peace and education for citizenship and democracy;
■ Health education;
■ Environmental sustainability;
■ The ageing population.

We would hope that CONFINTEA VI would give particular priority to:

■ Education for the whole person – avoiding disproportionate attention to any one of economic, social or cultural purposes;
■ Establishing a clear contract between individual, employers and the state – defining roles and responsibilities, especially in relation to funding;
■ Learner engagement – to support and share good practice in engaging learners in the design, management and quality assurance of adult learning;
■ Mobility, including access to learning about language and culture, and transfer of qualifications for a globally mobile population;
■ Access to resources – to develop better processes for exchanging and accessing educational resources across national barriers;
■ Comparative research – support the development of comparative research into adult learning.
■ Quality – to share expertise and develop appropriate quality assurance systems internationally.

General overview

The United Kingdom of Great Britain and Northern Ireland is made up of four nations: England, Wales, Scotland and Northern Ireland.[3] It has an area of 243,000 square km. and a population of 60 million.

The constitutional context

In 1997 the Conservative Government was replaced by a "New Labour" one, and the following decade has seen major, and unprecedented constitutional change, with a substantial devolution of functions to the Scottish Government and the Welsh Assembly Government.[4] Both Governments now have responsibility for education including large areas of adult education and training. Most remarkably, the ending of decades of conflict in Northern Ireland has also led to a transfer of much Government from Westminster to the new Northern Ireland Assembly, including education and training policy.

The devolution of many Government functions to Scotland, Wales and Northern Ireland has brought about significant divergence in educational policy and practice as they have adopted notably different approaches to key issues. The introduction of a form of proportional representation in these three (England retains "first past the post" electoral systems), has produced coalition and minority Governments which need to seek broader political consensus on major issues. The relative smallness of all three countries also means that elected politicians are much closer to constituents. As a result, some unpopular policies, like tuition fees for higher education, have been implemented differently in Scotland and Wales. (A map of national and regional boundaries within the UK is attached at the end of this chapter on page 21.)

The demographic context

The overall UK population continues to grow, although Scotland's population may be about the decline. There is also significant movement of population between regions, with a general drift of population (especially the more highly skilled) towards London and the South East),

3 This makes the UK the third largest country in the European Union, with 84 per cent of the population living in England
4 This was a major shift of power, although Scotland had always had a distinct education system, and some education functions were managed in Wales and Northern Ireland

and significant changes in age structures, especially in some rural areas. Of the 60.6 million[5] people in the UK in 2006, 77 per cent were adults.

Table 1 Population of the United Kingdom (millions)[6]

	1991	2001	2006	2011	2021
United Kingdom	57.4	59.1	60.6	62.8	67.2
England	47.9	49.5	50.8	52.7	56.8
Wales	2.9	2.9	3	3	3.2
Scotland	5.1	5.1	5.1	5.2	5.3
Northern Ireland	1.6	1.7	1.7	1.8	1.9

The main driver for population expansion is rising life expectancy. As a result of major improvements in the health of people aged 60–80, 21 per cent of the population is now over 59, and this proportion is expected to continue rising for the foreseeable future.

Although the UK population is overwhelmingly white, some 10 per cent of the population is from other ethnic groups, in general concentrated in large cities.[7] Scotland and Wales have a smaller proportion of non-white people. The overall minority ethnic populations at the 2001 Census are shown in Table 2.

Table 2 UK population by ethnic groups (2001)[8]

White British	88%
Other white (Irish, EU, White Commonwealth, US)	2.5%
Indian	1.8%
Pakistani	1.3%
Mixed Origin	1.2%
Black Caribbean	1.0%
Black African	0.8%
Bangladeshi	0.5%

In 2004 the European Union expanded to incorporate eight additional member states from Eastern Europe. The UK's decision to open its borders immediately to citizens of the new Member States led to a very large inflow of young adults (under 40) from Poland and other Eastern European countries.[9]

5 http://www.statistics.gov.uk/statbase/Expodata/Spreadsheets/D9657.xls

6 Source: Office for National Statistics; General Register Office for Scotland; Government Actuary's Department; Northern Ireland Statistics and Research Agency.

7 It is expected that Leicester will shortly become the first city to have a white minority

8 Self, Abigail and Linda Zealey (2007) *Social Trends*, London: National Statistics http://www.statistics. gov.uk/downloads/theme_social/Social_Trends37/Social_Trends_37.pdf

9 This is probably the largest single influx of immigrants in British history, estimated at around 500,000 people since 2004,and is not included in the 2001 census figures above.

Figure 1 Estimates of migration net flows by citizenship in the UK

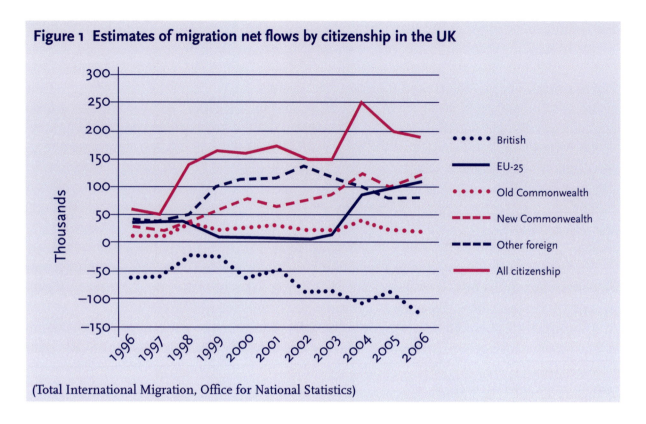

(Total International Migration, Office for National Statistics)

The economic context

Economically, the decade 1997–2007 saw the longest recorded period of continuous growth, allowing Government to make major increases in public expenditure, concentrated particularly on education, health, and overcoming social exclusion. The employment rate has grown to almost 75 per cent, one of the highest rates in the EU, and especially strongly among women. The rise in labour demand (and other factors) has led to an increase in effective retirement ages, with 1.3 million people still in work after State Pension Age in 2007.[10] It has also supported a surge of immigration from Eastern Europe following the expansion of the EU in 2004. This has led to a growing cultural, linguistic and ethnic diversity in the population, with migrants increasingly dispersing from urban enclaves to smaller towns and rural communities.

However, in early 2008 the UK economy was showing signs of slowing down. The 0.3 per cent rise in GDP in the first quarter was the weakest in three years and the annual growth rate had been revised downwards to 2.3 per cent.

The social context

On the social front, economic liberalisation has seen a widening of income gaps, and a slowing (perhaps to a halt) of the broad social mobility which characterised the previous

10 The earliest age at which an individual can draw a State Retirement Pension is currently 60 for women and 65 for men, but there is no obligation to retire at those ages and there are financial incentives to stay longer.

decades. While absolute poverty levels have declined, with a major reduction in child poverty,[II] social exclusion remains a policy concern.

Community cohesion has become a major focus of Government policy, fed particularly by concerns about international terrorism and the social exclusion of some ethnic and religious minority groups. The result was growing attention to the integration of new migrants, to the teaching of English and to citizenship education in schools.

There has also been a focus on reducing discrimination against particular groups. Established legislation outlawing discrimination on grounds of gender, race and disability has been extended to include age, religion and sexual orientation, and a new overarching Council for Equality and Human Rights has been created to oversee implementation, and support enforcement in all sectors, including education.

Government structures

In addition to the transfer of educational powers to the Devolved Administrations, one major structural change was the creation in 2007, of first time, of a Government Department in England with an exclusive focus on post school education, separate from the Department responsible for children and schools. This has created a sharper focus of policy attention on Further and Higher education.

In Scotland, immediately after devolution in 2000, lifelong learning was linked with enterprise in a new department of the Scottish Executive, although in 2007, within a re-organised Executive, all departments were abolished and all sectors of education are now included in a new education and lifelong learning directorate within the Scottish Government.

A further notable change has been the creation of a more centralised, and long term, process for policy development and monitoring across the UK Government. The former system of annual budgeting has been replaced by a three yearly "Comprehensive Spending Review" where Government reviews all Government programmes, and reallocates resources. These plans are then converted into "Public Service Agreements" (30 in the current cycle) which all Departments are expected to contribute to, with specified performance indicators for each, and detailed monitoring and annual review by the Treasury. Three of the current 30 PSAs are the responsibility of DIUS, but twelve have implications for adult learning.

The focus of Government policy

The decade has seen continuous change on many fronts, including in post-school education and training, and a growing interest among policymakers in international comparisons of structures, performance and innovation. By international standards, and by comparison with previous periods of UK policy history, the decade has seen an unprecedented level of policy

---

II According to the latest report, *Ending child poverty: everybody's business* (2008) some 600,000 children have been lifted out of relative poverty between 1998–99 and 2005–06 and the risk of children living in poverty fell from 26 to 22 per cent.

initiatives and structural changes, often led by policy "think tanks". Throughout the decade, Government policy has been driven by two interlinked objectives: to strengthen economic competitiveness through raising levels of skill and qualification, and to address social exclusion. The Government's view that the most effective way of overcoming social exclusion is to raise levels of employment, led initially to a strong "work first" strategy for reducing unemployment, but over time concern about low skills and sustainable employment has led to growing attention to training and skills.

A strong focus on evidence-based policy across all areas of Government has led to major research on the impact of education on productivity, employment and social inclusion. However, the growing evidence that a very large proportion of life chances are determined in the first three years of life means that although the increase in public expenditure has touched all types of learners it has been stronger in pre-school and early years services than in the education of adults.

The underlying direction of policy (in education as in other areas, and especially in England) has been towards individual choice, and a more market like model of services, in which individuals and employers are enabled to make their own decisions about their learning routes and choices, and buy suitable provision from a range of quality assured providers.

Whilst this focus on demand-side forces has a strong market dimension, it is also rooted in a growing understanding, supported by evidence from the government's Social Exclusion Unit, that a cause of intransigent social and economic deprivation has been the failure of public services to respond appropriately to the needs and demands of the poorest communities. Consulting service users, and tailoring service delivery to meet their needs, has been combined with a neo-liberal focus on individual choice, to create the concept of 'personalisation'. Imported into the adult learning arena, 'personalisation' also connotes listening better to learners' views and developing holistic approaches to work with learners with learning difficulties and disabilities.

Public expenditure has been concentrated on those with low skills, with the aim that they should be brought into the mainstream economy, enhancing both social inclusion and productivity. Individuals and employers are then expected to contribute a larger proportion of the costs of other kinds of provision. The expectation is that, over time, a more sophisticated mix of public, private and voluntary funding will lead to expansion in volume without a proportionate growth in public expenditure.

This approach has led to two complementary strands of development. On one hand institutions have been encouraged to become more responsive to demand, especially from employers. The largest, and most recent, of these initiatives has been the English *Train to Gain* programme which is discussed below. However, to date, the main driver of institutional behaviour has remained the systems of the Funding Councils, which distribute funding and steer policy on behalf of Government, and from whom Colleges get the majority of their funding. However, in Wales, all such funding bodies (other than the Higher Education Funding Council for Wales) have been incorporated directly into the Welsh Assembly Government.

A second strand has been a growth of information, advice and guidance (delivered both face to face and through online and telephone systems) to enable both individuals and employers to make informed use of the choices available. Here the latest proposals in England include a major development of career advice through a new and expanded Adult Advancement and Careers Service,[12] and a training brokerage service for employers through *Train to Gain*.

Government remains firmly committed to a voluntary approach to training for the existing workforce, with state intervention focused strongly on the supply side. The aim is to stimulate employer and individual demand by improving quality and the responsiveness of providers, and by supporting services to make training attractive to employers (including employer led Sector Skills Councils, reformed qualifications frameworks, and the employer focused Train to Gain programme). However, as the Government commissioned report on Skills (the "Leitch Report" of 2006) points out, the current poor qualification base is a result of this model, and Government has recently indicated that it will consider regulation at a future date if employers do not voluntarily increase their investment in training.

Figure 2 Qualifications held by the UK working-age population

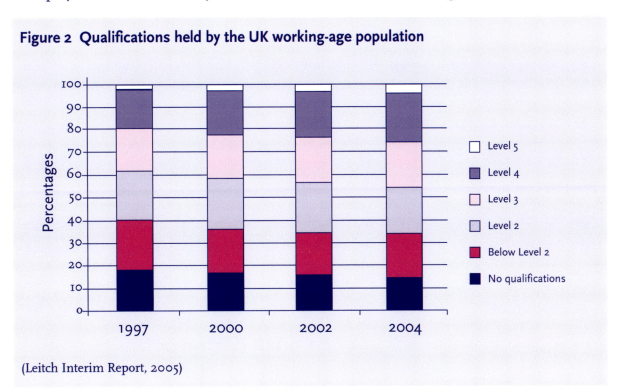

(Leitch Interim Report, 2005)

In Scotland, in 2007, the Scottish Government proposed a new skills strategy which not only seeks to address supply side issues but is also concerned with how skills are deployed in the workplace and work is in hand on specific initiatives in this area. A new organisation, Skills Development Scotland, has been established which brings together the careers advice services of Careers Scotland, the information and advice services of Learndirect Scotland and the training functions previously held by Scottish Enterprise, the Scottish economic development agency.

12 In Scotland similar functions are being delivered by a new body, Skills Development Scotland.

Educational structures

There is no distinct "adult learning sector" in the UK. Adult students participate in programmes in institutions of all sectors, including Further and Higher Education Institutions, Schools, Work based Learning Programmes, Voluntary and Community Organisations, and Local Authority Adult Education Services. Only the last of these is exclusively committed to adults, and it represents a very small proportion of the funding and hours studies, although it represents a significant proportion of overall student numbers.[13] The bulk of adult learning is provided through the FE and HE institutions.

Structurally, most of the management of public funding for adult learning is devolved to national Funding Councils. In England, these are the Higher Education Funding Council (HEFCE) for Higher Education; and the Learning and Skills Council (LSC) for "Further Education", which includes all vocational and non-vocational post-16 education and training. In Scotland, a single Scottish Funding Council is responsible for both Higher and Further Education, while Wales has a Funding Council for Higher Education (HEFCW), but since 2006 the funding of Further Education in Wales has been managed directly by the Welsh Assembly Government. These Funding Councils have played an increasingly interventionist part (working closely with Government) in delivering the objectives of economic and social policy. The situation is different in Northern Ireland (which is much smaller in population than the other countries) and there both further and higher education are funded through the Department for Employment and Learning, Northern Ireland (DELNI), advised by a non-statutory Northern Ireland Higher Education Council (NIHEC).

For most of the decade the major institutions of higher and further education have operated under a rigorous and demanding regime of regulation and quality assurance, designed to guarantee quality of provision for all learners, and value for money. As the quality of provision and routine data collection has improved, the quality assurance regimes have become more "light touch", concentrating external monitoring and support on those institutions with evident problems, and gradually transferring quality assurance responsibilities to bodies which are collectively "owned" by the institutions, rather than Government.

In order to ease transitions between phases of education, and create increased flexibility for learners and employers, a new National Qualification Framework has been created, with five levels from first level vocational qualifications to Postgraduate ones, and with three new Entry levels (with associated qualifications) for learners in the early stages of literacy and numeracy. All qualifications are now expressed in outcome terms.

Participation in formal education rose in the first half of the decade, and fell in the second, though the average numbers of hours studied has risen significantly as a result of the growing focus on longer qualification bearing courses. Overall, women outnumber men, although there remain concerns that they do not always participate in programmes of equal status, and women from some ethnic groups are seriously underrepresented. Participation among different minority ethnic communities varies widely, with people of black African and mixed

13 Most such students are enrolled on courses involving attendance for only 2 hours a week, usually for less than 20 weeks.

ethnic origin most likely to participate, and those of Pakistani and Bangladeshi origin least likely do so. There continues to be a strong social class bias in participation, with more than half of professional and managerial workers participating, compared to only one quarter of people in unskilled and semiskilled work doing so.

Reported motivation to learn remains high, although this is not entirely reflected in participation figures. A number of campaigns and other initiatives have been taken to stimulate interest and encourage take up, at national and local levels.

Because teachers of adults work in a wide variety of different institutions, there is no general teacher training programme or qualification. However, work has been undertaken to raise the quality of teaching force, with the introduction of mandatory qualifications for all teachers in further education (except in Scotland), and while teacher training for staff in Universities remains at the discretion of individual Universities, all have introduced schemes and these are generally taken up by new teaching staff.

There has been a great expansion of research into adult learning, carried out by Government, through Government sponsored (but independent) research centres, through Universities (mainly funded by the independent national Research Councils), and by agencies which combine research with development and policy activities. The quality and quantity of routine data collection has also improved, making it possible to track individual learners through their learning careers in further or higher education. The key findings include:

- the critical impact of pre-school learning on life chances;
- the importance of generic skills to employability;
- the importance of informal learning in the workplace;
- the limited impact of information technologies on education;
- the tendency of initiatives to widen participation to draw in those immediately below the entry threshold, rather than the more seriously excluded;
- that effective techniques and strategies for teaching numeracy and literacy are very different;
- that participation in adult learning has measurable positive impacts on social and political attitudes, and civic engagement;
- a national consultation on the support of informal learning.

One important source of evidence has been the major longitudinal cohort studies, the oldest of which has been running for 60 years, and can now generate data on lifecourse patterns. One important contribution has been the development of a set of principles of effective adult pedagogy derived from 100 separate research projects in the national Teaching and Learning Research Programme.

There have been a large number of innovations and initiatives in adult learning. Ongoing successful examples include the creation of:

- the Foundation Degree as a new vocational higher education qualification;
- a national education and training information service handling 8 million telephone enquiries and 20 million website hits a year;

■ a network of employer led Sector Skills Councils to oversee the development of skills and qualification policy for their occupational sectors;
■ structures for cross Government coordination of policy on older people;
■ Union Learning Representatives as workplace champions for learning.

Other major initiatives, which have not continued in their original form have included a "corporate university" for the National Health Service (the largest employer in Europe, and the creation of individual learner accounts to enable individuals to fund learning of their own choice.

Basic skills have been a major focus of policy intervention, with a Government expenditure of £3.5 billion since 2000, the development of national standards and associated qualifications in literacy and numeracy qualifications, large scale teacher training and promotional campaigns.

Commentary

A number of policy issues emerge from the UK experience in the last decade:

■ **The impact of policy change.** As the quality and quantity of evidence on underperformance in the education system, and the scale of skills problems has grown, Government has sought increasingly to intervene. One result of this is a growing volume of new initiatives and changes in institutional structures, which has increased the pressure on institutions and teaching staff to adapt to new processes and expectations. The current plan of the Department for Innovation, Universities and Skills identifies this as a potential risk to the implementation of policy, which needs to be managed carefully.
■ **The shift to a demand-led system.** Government has been seeking to move towards a more market like post-school education and training system, where the shape and volume of activity is driven more by employer and individual demand than by central planning. However, it recognises that a pure market model will evidently not deliver all the objectives of public policy, since the sum of individual and employer demand does not necessarily produce the ideal range of skills and knowledge for the long term economic interest. There is therefore a need to intervene in particular areas of market failure and to manage the shift towards a more market-led model carefully, building on the lessons learnt, for example, from the experience of Individual Learning Accounts, where demand exceeded expectations, placing strain both on public resources and on the ability to administer funding and avoid fraud.
■ **The academic–vocational divide.** Historically, academic qualifications in the UK (and especially England) have been seen by the public and media as superior in status to vocational ones, with vocational education seen as for those who "fail" in the mainstream system. Historically this perception has had damaging economic and social effects, and a major thrust of Government policy has been to change these perceptions and raise the status of vocational routes.
■ **The unintended effects of quality assurance systems.** In the 1990s concern to raise

standards led to the imposition of demanding national quality assurance regimes, and the setting of targets for learner participation and achievement. This produced evidence of improved performance throughout the system, but led to the loss of some less formal (and less easily measured) kinds of learning. There was widespread concern about the volume of work involved in operating these systems, and concern that these strategies, and the associated comparative "league tables" of courses and institutions, was leading institutions to select the most able students, and leading to "teaching to the test" rather that to the broader education of learners. More recently, in response to improvement, a "lighter touch" model was adopted for those institutions which had proved their capability to perform well, concentrating attention on those with difficulties.

■ **The "articulation" of the education and training system.** One major concern has been with the articulation of the overall system, and the needs of those who experience difficulties in making a successful transitions between phases of education (primary/secondary, 14–19, further/higher), and between different types of institution. A small, but significant, proportion of young people withdraw from education at the first opportunity (16 yrs) without formal qualifications, do not then continue in any form of education or training and do not find employment. There is great concern that these young people are effectively excluding themselves from full participation in a labour market which offers fewer opportunities for unskilled work. Following initiatives to coordinate the curriculum across institutional boundaries the UK Government has made a major investment in expanding vocational apprenticeships, and has announced its intention to make education, or employment with training, compulsory up to the age of 18 in England (although there are no plans to do this in Wales).

There is an ongoing debate about what kinds of institutional structure best help such young people. Four distinct types of institution provide for 16–19 year olds, but the availability of these in any locality is the result of a number of historical factors, rather than coordinated policy. Debate continues about how best to manage provision for this age range. Similar issues exist about the transition from secondary school and further education colleges into higher education, where Government's ambition to ensure that half of all young people participate in higher education before the age of 30 remains a serious challenge.

The development of a National Qualifications and Credit Framework for England, Wales and Northern Ireland also aims to improve coherence and flexibility across post-19 vocational qualifications (with the possibility of extending the framework to young people at a later date). The three countries are working closely to develop the framework, which will be aligned with the existing Scottish Credit and Qualifications Framework and the emerging European Qualifications Framework.

Framework for Credit and Qualifications also aims to provide coherence and flexibility across qualifications of all kinds (for adults as well as young people), but each of the four countries has taken rather different approaches to this.

■ **The role and future of non-vocational education for adults.** The UK has traditionally had a very extensive range of part-time adult education delivered by public and voluntary agencies at local level, and not generally leading to formal qualifications. The late 1990s saw rapid expansion of this, especially in further education colleges, driven by funding formulae which encouraged them to maximise participation by offering subsidised programmes, and by a policy to use such programmes to widen participation in education generally. However, the lack of a visible strong link between such programmes and Government's economic and social objectives led to repeated redefinition of the purposes and status of this work.[14] The intention of focusing public resources on vocational and qualification bearing courses was not that other kinds of courses should disappear, but that learners and employers should pay a larger share of the costs. However, the resulting rapid rises in fees for publicly supported non-vocational education have led to a dramatic fall in enrolments in such programmes. There is some evidence that some such provision has migrated from public sector to private or voluntary organisations, and the latest approach is to see this as part of a broader pattern of "informal adult learning", including public, private and voluntary sector activity. Government is currently undertaking a review of the purposes, funding and structures to support such activity.

- **The fluidity of ALE.** Over at least a decade, activity traditionally defined as "adult education" has moved, in response to changing levels of provision and fee policies, between public and private or voluntary sector agencies. For example, many of the physical education courses traditionally offered by Local Authority adult education services have been redefined as open access "leisure and recreation" provision, more strongly divided between high cost private sector services for richer participants, and publicly funded services for the poorer. Similarly, the focusing of public further education funds on priority qualifications has led to a decline in much "liberal" adult education, some of which has moved to agencies like the University of the Third Age. At the same time, broadcasters, museums and libraries are offering more informal and non-formal learning programmes. This makes the activity itself difficult to track and evaluate, and probably produces some shift in the nature of participation. The sector's diversity is one of its greatest strengths however it also makes it difficult to know whether the total volume, quality and accessibility of the resulting provision is comparable. The advent of new media/technologies means that learning is increasingly being delivered in new creative and innovative ways.

- **Qualifications and skills.** During the decade, policy has been increasingly influenced by a perception that the UK's economic competitiveness is being constrained by the level of skills in the adult population. In 2006, a major report, commissioned by Government from Lord Leitch, argued that the UK's skill base (measured by workforce qualifications) is seriously weaker than its competitors, and likely to deteriorate unless there is major policy change. This has strengthened the focus of Government policy on education and training which leads to specific vocational qualifications. There has been some academic debate about how adequately the qualification profile reflects the actual skills and capabilities of the workforce, and Scottish and Welsh policy has not adopted such a strong focus on formal qualifications.

---

14 Since 1997 this provision has had at least six different names ("adult and community learning", "non-vocational adult education", "personal and community development learning" etc), each trying to embody a broad and diverse range of programmes in a simple definition.

United Kingdom by nations and population

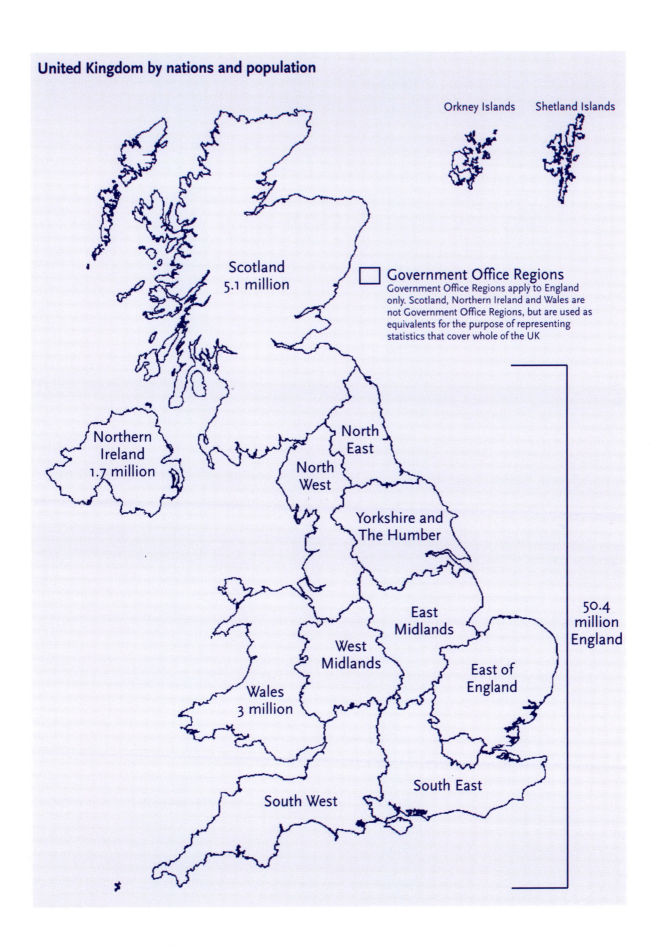

Orkney Islands

Shetland Islands

Scotland
5.1 million

Government Office Regions
Government Office Regions apply to England
only. Scotland, Northern Ireland and Wales are
not Government Office Regions, but are used as
equivalents for the purpose of representing
statistics that cover whole of the UK

Northern
Ireland
1.7 million

North
East

North
West

Yorkshire and
The Humber

East
Midlands

West
Midlands

East of
England

Wales
3 million

50.4
million
England

South East

South West

Adult learning and education in detail

1 Policy, legislation and financing

Devolution

One distinctive feature of the UK educational scene in the last decade has been the rapidity and frequency of change, including change in the structures of policy and governance. Following the 1997 General Election major areas of Government were devolved to elected assemblies in Scotland and Wales. In addition, the ending of decades of political conflict in Northern Ireland led to a similar devolution of powers to the new Northern Ireland Assembly. As a result, education and training policy now rests with the Scottish Executive and the Welsh and Northern Ireland Assemblies, while English policy remains in London. However, it is important to note the very large differences in size and population between the four countries (England has 84 per cent of the total population compared to 9 per cent in Scotland, 5 per cent in Wales and 3 per cent in Northern Ireland).

It would be a mistake to see education policy in the Devolved Administrations (DAs) as minor variants on the English model.[15] Since devolution, education policy has increasingly diverged on a number of issues. One reason for this is the relative size of the Devolved Administrations (DAs), which allows much closer relationships between services, education providers and Government. This effect has been strengthened by the use of proportional representation in elections in the DAs,[16] which has led to a more consensual approach to policymaking. Both these factors tend to produce a stronger sense of accountability to local communities. In general it has resulted in less heavy dependence on national targets and performance measures. While all four countries share a strong commitment to vocational skills and qualifications, Scotland and Wales have tended to place more stress on some of the social objectives of education policy.

15 And Scotland's education system had been distinct even prior to devolution
16 The Westminster Parliament, which retains policy responsibility in England, is still elected on a "first past the post" basis. In Wales, of the 60 elected members, the 40 constituency members are elected on a 'first past the post' basis, the remaining 20 regional members are elected using a form of proportional representation.

Scotland

The population of Scotland is 5.1 million (8.4 per cent of the UK total), heavily concentrated in the central belt between Glasgow and Edinburgh, and with large rural and remote areas with very dispersed populations.

In 2000, after devolution, the Scottish Executive established a new Enterprise and Lifelong Learning Department An early initiative was the creation of a task force on literacy and numeracy, which led to the publication of a strategy document in 2001 'Adult Literacy and Numeracy in Scotland', leading to increased funding for literacy an numeracy provision and the creation of Learning Connections within Communities Scotland (the Government agency for community development) to stimulate research, development and training and quality in literacy and numeracy provision.

In 2003 Scotland's new lifelong strategy, *Life through Learning: Learning through life*,[17] set a vision for a Scotland where people have the confidence, enterprise, knowledge, creativity and skills to participate in economic, social and civic life. It emphasised the role of informal and community learning in encouraging non-traditional learners into learning, as part of the process of ensuring that everyone has the chance to learn, irrespective of their background or current personal circumstances.

The implementation of the strategy saw a number of developments, most notably *Learndirectscotland*, which has the key role at a national level in promoting a culture of lifelong learning, while local authorities are responsible for encouraging local co-ordination of lifelong learning provision through the creation of community learning strategies and plans as part of a wider community planning partnership process. Careers Scotland, responsible for careers advice and guidance to young people and to adults was incorporated into Community Scotland, and some training responsibilities were held by the Government economic development agency, Scottish Enterprise.

These institutional arrangements, and stimulated by the earlier Osler report in 1999, *Communities: Change through Learning* encouraged the emphasis in recent years on seeing adult education as integral to community capacity building and the regeneration of communities.

The new Scottish Government proposed a new Scottish skills strategy in 2007 *Skills for Scotland, a lifelong Skills Strategy* which, among other things, heralded an attempt to simplify this structure through the creation of Skills Development Scotland which incorporates Learndirectscotland and Careers Scotland and some of the training functions of Scottish Enterprise. Learning Connections has now moved into the Lifelong Learning Directorate within the Scottish Government.

Wales

The population of Wales is 3 million (5 per cent of the UK total), heavily concentrated in the South, and with large rural areas with very dispersed populations.

17 Scottish Executive (2003) *Life through learning: learning through life: the lifelong learning strategy for Scotland*, Edinburgh: The Stationery Office

In 2001 the UK Government created a national Council ELW (Education and Learning Wales) as a strategic body responsible for planning and funding all post-16 education and training in Wales, except Higher Education. The Council was created at the same time, and through the same legislation, as the Learning and Skills Council in England. It was charged with delivering the post-16 educational element of the Welsh Assembly Government's strategy until 2010, as set out in its strategy document *The Learning Country*.[18] This strategy envisioned a substantial increase of learning participation and skills levels in Wales, through wider opportunities for learning, improved access (particularly for the socially disadvantaged) and better quality of provision across all sectors. The Learning Country strategy was updated in 2006 with the publication of *The Learning Country: Vision into Action*.

In 2007 the Welsh Assembly Government published *One Wales: a progressive agenda for the Government of Wales*.[19] Importantly, it presents "Learning for Life" as an inclusive concept from cradle to grave, rather than as a term to describe post-school education (as "lifelong leaning" is defined in England).

The Welsh Assembly Government's *Skills and Employment Action Plan 2002*[20] identified a range of measures to increase the skills of the existing workforce and help more adults to become economically active. Key measures here included the Basic Skills Strategy and the introduction of flexible packages of public support to meet the differing needs of individual employers.

At the end of 2006, the Welsh Assembly Government commissioned an Independent Review of the Mission and Purposes of Further Education in Wales. Sir Adrian Webb chaired the Review Team, and the resulting report (launched in December 2007) is known as the Webb Report.[21]

In January 2008, the Welsh Assembly Government launched a skills and employment strategy consultation (Skills That Work For Wales), which set out its response to the Leitch Review of Skills and the Webb review. Although it maintained a focus on social justice, the consultation document indicated a policy shift towards employer-led provision. The Welsh Assembly Government is due to publish its skills and employment strategy in the summer of 2008 and to consult upon its strategy for Adult and Community Learning in the autumn of 2008.

In Wales, one result of devolution has been a stronger emphasis on the community benefits of learning; a stronger focus on collaboration and partnership, rather than competition between institutions; a stronger emphasis on the role of the third sector in provision; and a greater sensitivity to the needs of particular communities (including rural areas, and declining former industrial ones). Wales has also taken a distinct approach to qualifications, with the creation of the "Welsh Baccalaureate" and a generally more cautious

18 National Assembly for Wales (2001) *The Learning Country: a paving document: a comprehensive and lifelong learning programme to 2010 in Wales*, Cardiff: Welsh Office
19 http://news.bbc.co.uk/1/shared/bsp/hi/pdfs/27_06_07_onewales.pdf
20 National Assembly for Wales (2001) *Skills and employment action plan for Wales 2002: a consultation document*, Cardiff: Welsh Office
21 Its published title is: *Promise and Performance: The Report of the Independent Review of the Mission and Purpose of Further Education in Wales in the context of the Learning Country: Vision into Action*.

approach to some of the initiatives (like *Train to Gain*) which feature in English policy. Wales also faces a particular challenge because it is, by Statute, a bilingual country, and education and training services must be available in both English and Welsh.

Northern Ireland

The population of Northern Ireland is 1.8 million (3 per cent of the UK total). Government powers returned to Northern Ireland in 2007, when the elected Northern Ireland Assembly took control, following the end of decades of political conflict.

In Northern Ireland, the 1998 report *Lifelong Learning: A new learning culture for all*[22] presented a package of measures and associated funding to fulfil the Government's strategic aim of developing and sustaining a culture of lifelong learning. For example, the 'Partnership Fund' assisted FE colleges in establishing local partnerships inclusive of all major interests e.g. employers, District Councils, Chambers of Commerce, community organisations, trade unions, and providers of education and training at every level. The partnerships aimed to take forward innovative approaches, that brought teaching and learning to those who would not ordinarily use further education.

More recent documents *Success Through Skills* (2006) and *Success Through Skills Progress Report* (2007) have shifted the policy focus towards skills and have set four broad themes for adult learning providers:

- Understanding the demand for skills
- Improving the skills level of the workforce
- Improving the quality and relevance of education and training
- Tackling the skills barrier to employment and employability

1.1 Legislative and policy frameworks of ALE in England

1.1.1 The legislative and policy environment of ALE since 1997

Adult learning has taken on a much higher profile in the UK since CONFINTEA V and in the past decade a plethora of policy documents have shaped the political landscape. Four Acts of Parliament directly affecting post-school education have come into force, and two further Bills are in progress through Parliament at the time of writing (see Annex 2). In addition, there have been national inquiries into Higher Education, Further Education, Basic Skills, Widening Participation, Skills and Competitiveness. There have been formal consultations,

22 Department for Education and Training (1998) *Lifelong Learning: a new learning culture for all*, Belfast: The Stationery Office

with the general public and with specialised audiences on more technical issues, and a number of Green and White Papers.[23]

Policy development over the decade is here described in relation to the three terms of the Labour Government, each of which has sought to build on its predecessor, but has had a distinctive focus.

1997–2000

In June 1997, shortly before CONFINTEA V, and immediately after its election, the incoming UK Government rejoined UNESCO. It also established a **National Advisory Group for Continuing Education and Lifelong Learning**, to provide advice on adult learning policy. Within the first six months it produced the report, *Learning for the 21st Century*,[24] which recommended the creation of a new strategic framework of lifelong learning for all, to include both compulsory and post-compulsory education. The Group's proposals sought to create a fundamental attitude change towards learning in individuals, employers and Government. Its proposals would give emphasis to widening access and to the recognition of the home, community and workplace as key places for learning. The report advised that a Government White Paper should set out the vision and rationale for lifelong learning along with a step-by-step outline of targets and practical goals to achieve.

In 1998, the Government responded with a Green Paper on lifelong learning entitled, *The Learning Age: a renaissance for a new Britain*.[25] Although it was only a consultative paper, it enthusiastically proposed a 'Learning Age' in which adults were encouraged to enter and re-enter learning at every point in their lives. The main proposals for England were to:

- *expand further and higher education to provide for an extra 500,000 places by 2020;*
- *make it easier for firms and individuals to learn by creating a "University for Industry" (UfI) for launch in late 1999;*
- *set up individual learning accounts to encourage people to save to learn, and begin by allocating £150 million to support investment in learning accounts by one million people;*
- *invest in young people so that more continue to study beyond age 16;*
- *double help for basic literacy and numeracy skills amongst adults to involve over 500,000 adults a year by 2002;*
- *widen participation in and access to learning both in further, higher, adult and community education (including residential provision), and through the UfI;*

---

23 **National inquiries** are normally commissioned by Government, to examine major policy issues; **Consultative documents**: invite views on a key issue without necessarily putting forward specific proposals; **Green Papers** are Government consultative documents containing policy proposals for broad public discussion; **White Papers** outline formal policy proposals for planned legislation or regulation; **Bills and Acts of Parliament**, and Regulations are formal legislation creating bodies, changing constitutional or funding arrangements, and creating duties and powers. These may stem from Government initiatives, or be a response to agreed policies and regulations from the European Union.

24 Fryer (1997) *Learning for the Twenty-First Century: First Report of the National Advisory Group for Continuing Education and Lifelong Learning*, http://www.lifelonglearning.dfee.gov.uk/nagcell/index.htm

25 DfEE (1998) *The Learning Age: a renaissance for a new Britain*, London: The Stationery Office.

- *raise standards across teaching and learning after the age of 16 through our new Training Standards Council by ensuring implementation of the Dearing committee's standards proposals, and by inspection in further and adult education;*
- *set and publish clear targets for the skills and qualifications we want to achieve as a nation;*
- *work with business, employees and their trade unions to support and develop skills in the workplace;*
- *build a qualification system which is easily understood, gives equal value to both academic and vocational learning, meets employers' and individuals' needs and* promotes the highest standards.

(DfEE, 1998, p.15)

The Learning Age received wide public support with over 3,000 responses submitted, a great majority of which were positive. Stakeholders especially welcomed the vision set out by the then Secretary of State for Education and Employment, David Blunkett:

As well as securing our economic future, learning has a wider contribution. It helps make ours a civilised society, develops the spiritual side of our lives and promotes active citizenship. Learning enables people to play a full part in their community. It strengthens the family, the neighbourhood and consequently the nation. It helps us fulfil our potential and opens doors to a love of music, art and literature. That is why we value learning for its own sake as well as for the equality of opportunity it brings.

(DfEE, 1998 p.7).

Although important and large-scale initiatives stemmed from *The Learning Age*, not all of them have survived intact. For example, Individual Learning Accounts, which were designed to stimulate individual demand for learning, expanded so rapidly that the scheme exceeded the planned budget and the capacity of its administrative and financial systems, and had to be suspended in England (though they continued in some form in Wales, Scotland and for employees of the National Health Service).[26] Another initiative was the *University for Industry* (UfI), designed as a parallel institution to the *Open University*, to provide on-line learning to people at work or seeking to study at levels below university. UfI has survived, though it has gone through several different remits in the years since its inception, and is now a provider of online short courses through local learning centres, and of career and educational advice by telephone and online.

A further success stemming from the Green Paper has been work with trade unions, including the creation and financing of Union Learning Representatives as workplace champions for learning, and the Union Learning Fund, to promote trade unions' support in the creation of a learning society. In the decade since the work started more than 20,000 trades unionists have become union learning representatives, encouraging colleagues back into learning. A final initiative from the *Learning Age* was the Adult and Community Learning

---

26 See section 3.2.

Fund, aimed at widening participation in learning through developing and sustaining innovative adult learning projects. As a result of the Fund, around 600 large and small projects focused at adult who do not normally participate in education received funds ranging from a few hundred pounds to over £100,000. The National Institute of Adult Continuing Education (NIACE) and the Basic Skills Agency (BSA) jointly managed the fund until it was closed in March 2004.

Adult literacy has been a major policy concern for over a decade, and in its early years, the incoming Government commissioned Sir Claus Moser to conduct an inquiry into the issue. In 1999 his report *A Fresh Start – improving literacy and numeracy*[27] highlighted the fact that 7 million adults in England were functionally illiterate and that one in five adults had very low numeracy levels. The report recommended an English national strategy that would:

- set a nationwide target to reduce by half the number of functionally illiterate adults of working age by 2010;
- create a new system of basic skills qualifications;
- develop a framework to secure quality provision;
- establish an entitlement to learn and improve basic skills free of charge.

The English Government responded to the Moser Report with *Better Basic Skills*,[28] which announced a national basic skills curriculum based on new standards, and the creation of a new qualification for new teachers of basic skills.

Soon after, in 1999, the Government published *Learning to Succeed: A new framework for post-16 learning*,[29] the first in a series of White Papers focused on skills. The document identified that the system for managing post-compulsory learning was inconsistent and confusing and proposed to establish a new body, the Learning and Skills Council (LSC) for England, to drive forward quality and access of all post-16 learning in a coherent and responsive way. The remit of the new Council was to plan, fund, monitor, improve and drive up demand in post-16 learning. In its first letter to the Council, the then Secretary of State, David Blunkett said,

> It is the first time that public body has had a statutory duty placed upon it to encourage participation in learning, and I look to the Council to keep this sense of purpose at the heart of all its work and aim to make a real difference to people's lives.[30]

The remit also made the Council responsible of advising and overseeing a set of post-16 National Learning Targets for England. These included:

27 Moser, Sir Claus (1999) A fresh start: Improving literacy and numeracy, http://www.lifelonglearning.co.uk/mosergroup/
28 DfEE (1999) Better, Basic Skills, http://www.lifelonglearning.co.uk/betterbasics/leaflet.pdf
29 DfEE (1999) Learning to Succeed: a new framework for post-16 learning, London: The Stationery Office.
30 Blunkett, David (2000) *The Learning and Skills Council: Strategic Priorities*, London.

■ raising the percentage of adults with Level 3 qualifications[31] from 45 per cent to 50 per cent by 2002

■ raising the percentage of adults with a Level 4 qualification from 26 per cent to 28 per cent.

In July 2000, the *Learning and Skills Act* became law, establishing the Learning and Skills Council (LSC), a new body to secure and actively promote provision of education and training for all post-16 learning outside of higher education. The Act gave the LSC the responsibility to manage and provide funding for further education colleges, work based learning providers, adult education institutions and voluntary organisations, as well as the task of encouraging employers and individuals to participate in learning. The legislation also provided the new body with a local presence through 47 local councils. Further responsibilities set by the Act were: provision of information, advice and guidance services, provision of equal opportunities and provision catered to the needs of people with learning difficulties.

The Act also established a new Adult Learning Inspectorate to continually examine the quality of further education for people aged 19 or over; training provided wholly or partly on employers' premises for people aged over 16; and training funded under the 1973 Employment and Training Act.[32]

Also within this period (1998–2000) a *Skills Task Force* operated under the chairmanship of Chris Humphries to advise the Secretary of State for Education and Skills on the nature of skills shortages, skill gaps and assist him on the development of a national skills agenda. The Task Force included employer and trade union representatives as well as education and training providers.

2001–2004

In March 2001, the Government began its second term of office by publishing its response to the Moser report. *Skills for Life: The national strategy for improving adult literacy and numeracy skills*[33] aimed to improve the literacy and numeracy skills of 750,000 adults by 2004 through a promotional campaign and reinforcing the entitlement to free training in basic skills. The strategy also identified priority groups for targeting. These were unemployed adults and welfare benefit claimants, offenders, public sector employees, people who do not speak English as a first language and low-skilled in employment.

In 2003, Government published its first skills White Paper, *21st Century Skills: Realising our Potential*.[34] The paper aimed to strengthen the UK's position as one of the world's leading economies by ensuring individuals have the necessary skills to make them employable and adaptable and that employers had the right skills to support their businesses. The White Paper sets out a new understanding of how the Government, employers and individuals

---

31 Broadly equivalent to ISCED 3

32 The Adult Learning Inspectorate merged with OFSTED in 2007.

33 DfEE (2001) *Skills for Life: the national strategy for improving adult literacy and numeracy skills*, Nottingham.

34 DfEE (2003) *21st Century Skills: realising our potential: individuals, employers, nation*, London: Stationery Office.

would create a demand-led education and training system, which would raise the skills of the nation. Key proposals in the paper include:

■ A new entitlement for adults without 'Level 2'[35] qualifications to receive free education and training to help them reach this standard and the introduction of a new adult learning grant for learners studying full time up to this level;
■ new opportunities for adults to gain qualifications in technician and higher craft and trade skills;
■ offering basic skills in Information and Communication Technology (ICT) as a third area of adult basic skills alongside literacy and numeracy within the *Skills for Life* programme
■ lifting the age cap for Modern Apprenticeships[36] so that people over the age of 25 could learn skilled trades;
■ safeguarding the budget for leisure, culture and community learning;
■ reforming adult information, advice and guidance services to help adults into learning.

The White Paper also announced the creation of 23 Sector Skills Councils (SSCs) to represent a new voice for employers and employees. SSCs are independent employer led organisations with a remit to identify solutions to the skills needs of different economic sectors and generate additional demand for skills and training.

In 2004, the controversial *Higher Education Act* became law in England. The Act aimed to increase funding for Universities by introducing, for the first time in the UK, a student fee. It enabled Universities to charge full time undergraduate students up to £3,000 a year, provided that the institution satisfied a new regulator (the Office of Fair Access) that it had adequate arrangement for supporting poorer students, and those from non-traditional backgrounds. To avoid the new regime from discouraging poorer people applying for higher education, a loan scheme was created, under which full-time students could borrow to finance their living costs and defer payment of the loan until they were earning more than £15,000 p.a. However part-time students were not included in the loan scheme and continue to pay up-front fees. The Scottish Executive, and the Welsh Assembly Government chose not to introduce fees, although in Scotland a charge was introduced for all students specifically to pay for support for poorer students.

2005–2008

In 2005 the further skills strategy White Paper was published, *Skills: Getting on in business, getting on at work.*[37] The document built on the 2003 White Paper and proposed to put employers' needs at the centre of the design and delivery of training. It announced the

---

35 Regarded as the minimum level of skills for successful working in a modern society, a Level 2 qualification is broadly comparable to NVQ Level 2, GNVQ Intermediate, and GCSE grades A* to C and ISCED Level 2.
36 Launched in 1993, Modern Apprenticeships were designed 'by employers for employers' to help address the decline in numbers in work-based training at Level 3 NVQ and above
37 DfES (2005) *Skills: Getting on in business, getting on at work*, http://www.dfes.gov.uk/skillsstrategy/uploads/documents/Skills%20WP%20Part%201.pdf

implementation of a *National Employer Training Programme* as the strategy to give employers a greater say in how public funds are used to address business priorities. In return for free and flexibly funded training, employers were expected to allow employees time at work to undertake their studies. For individual learners it reinforced the Government commitment for any low-skilled adult to get free training to achieve a first full Level 2 qualification. It also gave the Skills for Life programme the new target of 2.25 million adults to achieve literacy and numeracy qualifications by 2010.

By 2005, ALE policy had shifted focus from a broad definition of lifelong learning to a much stronger focus on learning for employability, skills and work. Although the 2005 White Paper acknowledged that for many people, learning is also a great source of pleasure and interest, it only agreed to reserve a budget of £210m p.a. for such work. This was equivalent to the sum being spent at that time on such programmes by Local Authorities (whose budgets were absorbed into the LSC's), and this sum was not subsequently adjusted for inflation.

Also in 2005, the Government published the Foster review, *Realising the Potential – a review of the future of FE colleges*.[38] It reinforced Government policy by recommending that colleges should direct their energies more strongly towards improving employability and providing economically valuable skills to their students. It also called for a strong focus on quality improvement, and proposed a national workforce development strategy for FE teachers.

In the following year, 2006, two important skills policy documents were published. The first was a new White Paper *Further Education: Raising Skills, Improving Life Chances*[39] published in response to the Foster Review. This presented a strategy to make the FE system fit for the purpose of up-skilling the adult workforce with the competences and qualifications that employers want and to prepare adults for productive and rewarding employment. It placed this economic mission at the heart of the FE sector's role. The White Paper also set a new entitlement to free training for young people up to the age of 25 to achieve a Level 3 (ISCED 3), and announced a new service, *Train to Gain*, to help employers to improve the skills of their employees, unlock talent, and drive improved business performance, with subsidised training for basic skills and individuals studying for their first full Level 2 qualification. Train to Gain is to be accompanied with a Learner Account programme, to give individuals greater choice and control over their own learning. The document envisioned that by 2010, 40 per cent of the adult skills budget would be allocated through the *Train to Gain* programme. The White Paper also proposed the creation of a single Quality Improvement Agency to lead the improvement of teaching and learning in FE, and introduced a Continuing Professional Development (CPD) requirement for all staff.

Secondly in December 2006, the Government published the Leitch Report, *Prosperity for all in the global economy: World Class Skills*,[40] one of the most influential documents of this decade. The report provided an account of the UK's current skills landscape, making heavy

38 Foster, Sir Andrew (2005) *Realising the potential: a review of the future role of further education colleges*, http://www.dcsf.gov.uk/furthereducation/uploads/documents/REALISING06.pdf.
39 DfES (2006) *Further Education: Raising Skills, Improving Life Chances*, http://www.official-documents.gov.uk/document/cm67/6768/6768.pdf
40 Leitch (2006) *Prosperity for all in the global economy- world class skills*, http://www.dfes.gov.uk/skillsstrategy/uploads/documents/Leitch%20Review.pdf

use of OECD data to demonstrate the low level of skills in the UK workforce (as measured by formal qualifications). It recommended a major strategic change, and investment to move the UK into the top quartile of OECD countries in terms of adult qualifications by 2020, and proposed a new set of targets for the UK:

- 95 per cent of adults to achieve the basic skills of functional literacy and numeracy, an increase from levels of 85 per cent literacy and 79 per cent numeracy in 2005;
- exceeding 90 per cent of adults qualified to at least Level 2, an increase from 69 per cent in 2005. A commitment to go further and achieve 95 per cent as soon as possible;
- shifting the balance of intermediate skills from Level 2 to Level 3. Improving the esteem, quantity and quality of intermediate skills. This means 1.9 million additional Level 3 attainments over the period and boosting the number of Apprentices in England to 400,000 a year;
- exceeding 40 per cent of adults qualified to Level 4 and above, up from 29 per cent in 2005, with a commitment to continue progression.

The Review argued that responsibility for achieving targets should be shared between Government, employers and individuals. It advised that all three stakeholders would need to increase action and investment and focus their efforts on economically valuable skills. Leitch recommended that the way forward was to build on existing structures while at the same time modifying the system to make it more demand-led and responsive to future market needs. Key elements of the plan were mechanisms to make provision more responsive to employer need, through the *Train to Gain* service, and to make it more responsive to individual learners, through Learning Accounts, giving individuals the power to spend on their own education and training.

In 2007 Gordon Brown replaced Tony Blair as Prime Minister. One of his first acts in office was to divide the Department for Education and Skills into two departments: the Department for Children, Schools and Families and the Department for Innovation, Universities and Skills. For the first time in England adult learning was given a separate Government department.

The English Government then published its response to Leitch, the White Paper, *World Class Skills: Implementing the Leitch Review of Skills in England.*[41] It proposed a "skills revolution" to close skills gaps at every level by 2020, through a demand-led system where the needs of adult learners and employers were given priority. Adult learners would be given priority through Skills Accounts, which would give individuals greater ownership and choice over learning. The employers' role would be strengthened through a new UK Commission for Employment and Skills and through an increased level of investment in *Train to Gain* (over £1 billion p.a. by 2010/2011), where employers would receive individual brokerage support to identify and source training to meet their particular needs, and Government subsidy for training in priority areas.

41 DIUS (2007) World Class Skills: Implementing the Leitch Review of Skills in England, http://www.dfes.gov.uk/skillsstrategy/uploads/documents/World%20Class%20Skills%20FINAL.pdf

'*World Class Skills*' and the Welfare Reform Green Paper: '*In work, better off: next steps to full employment*' both published in July 2007 set out a new offer for individuals with DIUS and DWP working jointly to ensure that the skills and employment systems work more effectively for the benefit of the customer. The integration of employment and skills policies aimed to help more workless and low skilled people move into sustainable employment, progress in work, and develop their skills, and thus contribute both to improvement in the UK's productivity and in social inclusion. '*Opportunity, Employment and Progression: making skills work*' published on 26 November 2007 set out the next steps in developing an integrated employment and skills services, and was followed in June 2008 by the joint DIUS/DWP paper '*Work Skills*' which describes steps to create an integrated employment and skills service that is more responsive to the needs of both individuals and employers

A major concern of the paper was with how to raise employer ambition and investment in skills at all levels. To tackle demand, Sector Skills Councils were given the remit to raise demand and articulating future skills needs. Another mechanism developed to raise ambition was the Skills Pledge, a public and voluntary commitment by employers to support their staff to achieve basic literacy and numeracy and a first full Level 2 qualification. Legislation was planned to strengthen the already existing funding entitlement for adults to free training in basic skills and first full Level 2 qualifications. Finally and importantly, Government committed itself to review the employer response to the strategy in 2010 in order to consider whether some form of compulsory training levy on employers was necessary, something which UK Government has resisted since the 1970s as an unnecessary interference with the market.

Parliament implemented these plans through the Further Education and Training Act 2007. This allowed further education colleges to award their own foundation degrees (ISCED 5B). Previously, only universities held degree-awarding powers. Foundation degrees are available in England, Wales and Northern Ireland. The Act also replaced the 47 local LSC Councils with nine regional ones and allowed the London Skills and Employment Board to direct more closely the strategic focus of the LSC in London.

In early 2008, the Department for Innovation, Universities and Skills published a consultation entitled, *Informal Adult Learning – Shaping the Way Ahead*.[42] The document focuses on what the European Union defines as intentional informal and non-formal learning undertaken for personal fulfilment and not necessarily linked to qualifications or employment. Stakeholders were asked to help formulate mechanisms to determine the best use of existing public funds and support for private initiatives. This was the first Government paper since The Learning Age in 1998 that focused on informal and non-formal education for adults.

In March 2008, the Government announced further details of the machinery of government changes, which included the dismantling of the Learning and Skills Council. The consultation document, *Raising Expectations: enabling the system to deliver*[43] announced

42 DIUS (2008) *Informal Adult Learning – Shaping the Way Ahead*, http://www.dius.gov.uk/publications/ DIUS_adu_lea_bro_an_05%208.pdf
43 DIUS (2008) *Raising Expectations: Enabling the system to deliver*, http://www.dfes.gov.uk/consultations/ downloadableDocs/Raising%20Expectations%20pdf.pdf

plans to replace the LSC by 2010 with two different bodies: the Young People's Learning Agency looking after 16–18 provision and the Skills Funding Agency looking at 19 plus provision. The latter would manage all adult learning outside higher education, and would have a funding rather than a planning remit. Most provision for adults would be routed through an expanded Train to Gain service, and through a re-introduction of Skills Accounts.

Furthermore, at the time of writing, the *Education and Skills Bill* is going through its second reading[44] in the House of Commons. If enacted, it will, for the first time, make it illegal for anyone under 18 to not be in either full time education or employment with a significant training component. It will also formally create the entitlement for adults to not only free training in basic literacy and numeracy skills but also to achieve a first full level 2 qualification (ISCED 2).

1.1.2 The priority goals for ALE in England

Upskilling and labour productivity

In adult learning, the primary aim of the UK Government from 2007 to 2011 is raising the productivity of the workforce.[45] The Government has noted that productivity is low compared to other major industrial competitors and skills are identified as one of the five key drivers of productivity. Consequently upskilling the working age population in order to raise productivity levels is the foremost priority affecting the adult education arena. The Government wants to make the UK a "world leader on skills" raising it to the upper quartile of OECD rankings by 2020, and it sees adult learning as at the core of the strategy to achieve this vision.[46] The following targets have been set for 2010 in England:

■ 597,000 people of working age to achieve a first Level 1 or above literacy qualification, and 390,000 to achieve a first entry level 3 or above numeracy qualification.
■ 79 per cent of working age adults qualified to at least full Level 2
■ 56 per cent of working age adults qualified to at least full Level 3
■ 130,000 apprentices to complete the full apprenticeship framework in 2010–11 – 34 per cent of working age adults qualified to Level 4 and above by 2011
■ Increase participation in Higher Education towards 50 per cent of those aged 18 to 30 with growth of at least a percentage point every two years to the academic year 2010–11

(Public Service Agreement 2, 2007)

44 A Bill is a proposal for a new law, or a proposal to change an existing law that is presented for debate before Parliament. Bills are introduced in either the House of Commons or House of Lords for examination, discussion and amendment. When both Houses have agreed on the content of a Bill it is then presented to the reigning monarch for approval (known as Royal Assent). Once Royal Assent is given a Bill becomes an Act of Parliament and is law.
45 HM Government (2007) *PSA Delivery Agreement 1: Raise the productivity of the UK economy*, http://www.hm-treasury.gov.uk/media/3/A/pbr_csr07_psa1.pdf
46 It should be noted that this commitment has not been adopted with such enthusiasm in Scotland and Wales, where skills is seen as only one of several factors affecting productivity.

Government is therefore prioritising funds within the post-19 education budget towards those with low-level skills, those studying to achieve a first or higher qualification rather than a lower or equivalent one and those currently unemployed. There is an explicit focus on increasing the number of adults with Level 2 qualifications because this level is seen as the basic platform for sustainable employment and progression.

Stimulating demand for learning through employer engagement and provision of economically valuable skills

A major Government priority is to stimulate demand for work related learning, and it expects employers to support this, both in terms of financing and time off from work to study, in order to achieve the adult qualification targets. Since the 1970s, Government has sought to achieve this on a voluntary basis, seeking employer cooperation through improving the supply side, rather than through regulation of the demand for skills or qualifications. However, the Leitch Review proposed that Government should review in 2010 whether the voluntary approach to employer investment in skills has been successful, and the Government has confirmed that it will then consider the possibility of some form of compulsion.

Government has also sought to give employers a greater say in the design and availability of qualifications, through the creation of the national network of Sector Skills Councils, and the employer led UK Commission for Employment and Skills (formerly the Sector Skills Development Agency and National Employment Panel) which supports them (see 1.1 above). UKCES will produce a five-year strategy and operational plan for the employment and skills systems. Additionally the Government has developed a Skills Pledge whereby businesses make a public (though not a legally binding) commitment to support their staff to gain basic skills and competencies. Government funding is available for training that helps adults gain certificates in literacy and numeracy skills and their first full Level 2 qualification. . Finally, to ensure that the formal vocational qualifications system has the flexibility to meet all employers' training needs, the Government has introduced a scheme offering a range of ways to accredit employers' training, where it meets the standards required of regulated qualifications.

The major plank of the Government's attempt to engage employers, is the *Train to Gain* service, which provides an impartial brokerage service to help employers identify skills needs and procure appropriate training. The service examines skills needs at all levels, and aims to help employers find training which meets those needs at time and place to suit their needs. Employers pay for much of this training, but Government subsidises (up to 100 per cent in some cases) training where it also contributes to Government objectives (*Skills for Life* or Level 2 qualifications). Between launch in April 2006 and spring 2008 Train to Gain has:

- Engaged over 92,000 employers of which 75 per cent were 'hard to reach' employers ;
- Enabled almost 455,000 employees to begin learning programmes;
- Delivered over 211,00 qualification achievements including over 23,000 *Skills for Life* achievements and over 186,000 first full Level 2,

The evaluation of the first year of *Train to Gain* found that:

■ Colleges varied greatly in their willingness and speed of response, especially to demand for programmes which did not attract LSC subsidy;

■ Processes were seen as unduly bureaucratic;

■ There was an undue focus on Skills for Life and Level 2 qualifications. This was consistent with broader Government priorities, but limited subsidised responsiveness to employers' needs;

■ A perception that the service was primarily about delivering free training, rather than brokering appropriate training;

■ Difficulty in engaging higher education institutions in providing training;

■ Insufficient focus on the recruitment of Apprenticeships

■ Significant regional variation in take up and performance.

■ The service attracted a high proportion of older learners than those generally receiving training at work.

■ 77 per cent of learner were either extremely or very satisfied with their experience.

In response, Government published, in November 2007, *Train to Gain: a Plan for Growth* laying out its proposals for the future development of the service as the central plank of Government investment in the learning of the adult workforce. These included:[47]

■ doubling the budget to £1 billion (1/3 of the further education budget) in 2010–11.[48]

■ the LSC to support and monitor the performance of further education providers in responding to employer demand;

■ strengthen employer brokerage, providing this from 2009 through Business Links (the national support service for small business) and with enhanced sector based expertise;

■ maintain an expectation that over half of employers involved will be "hard to reach" (with little or no previous training record);

■ a specific fund of £90 million over 3 years for management training for senior staff in small firms;

■ increased flexibility in the kind of courses and learners who can be included in Train to Gain funding.

Evaluations of the second year of Train to Gain were considerably more positive showing that among those participating:

■ 80 per cent of employers were satisfied with the skills brokerage service, and especially with the impartial advice and local knowledge

■ 78 per cent of employers who had taken up training through the service would recommend it to other employers, and 82% gave an overall satisfaction score of 8 or more out of 10.

■ 77 per cent of learners were 'extremely satisfied' or 'very satisfied' with their Train to Gain experience.

47 www.dius.gov.uk/publications/Train-to-Gain-Executive-Summary.pdf
48 DIUS and DCSF (2007) Annexe B, LSC Grant Letter: 2008-0, http://www.dius.gov.uk/publications/LSC-Grant-Letter-2008-09.pdf

■ 51 per cent of employers reported some increase in staff productivity, 42 per cent reported an impact on the bottom line, 25% said that the training had supported the introduction of new products or services, and 22% said absenteeism had reduced.

National Inquiry into Lifelong Learning

There have been a series of major inquiries into aspects of education policy over the decade, and in the early years of the New Labour Government a National Advisory Group for Continuing Education and Lifelong Learning was created.

Ten years later, in 2007, NIACE (National Institute of Adult Continuing Education) decided to sponsor a further national[49] inquiry into the future of lifelong learning. The 12 Commissioners, chaired by Sir David Watson, are independent of both NIACE and Government, and are considering the implications of major social and economic trends for the demand for and supply of lifelong learning. In the first year, they have commissioned a series of discussion papers, convened expert seminars and invited public views on a series of key themes:[50]

■ Prosperity, employment and work
■ Demography and social structure
■ Well-being and happiness
■ Migration and communities
■ Technological change
■ Poverty reduction
■ Citizenship and belonging
■ Crime and social exclusion
■ The roles of the public, private and voluntary sectors
■ Environmental sustainability

In the second year, the Commission will refine its proposals for action, with a view to influencing public policy, both in the next General Election, and the Comprehensive Spending Review in 2010.

1.1.3 How is ALE organised?

In 2007, for the first time, an English Government Department solely concerned with post-16 education was created. The former Department for Education and Skills was split into a Department for Children, Schools and Families and a new Department for Innovation, Universities, Skills and Science (DIUS). Although there is no department with the word "adult" (or "education") in its title, DIUS has a Ministers for Lifelong Learning, Further and Higher Education; and one for Skills; both with responsibilities for adult learning. This has not happened in the Devolved Administrations, which have distinct structures of their own.

---

49 Formally covering only England and Wales, since NIACE's remit does not extend to Scotland or Northern Ireland, but evidence is being gathered, and dialogue taking place throughout the UK.
50 www.niace.org.uk/lifelonglearninginquiry

In Wales, the Department for Children, Education, Lifelong Learning and Skills (DCELLS) was created after the 2007 WAG election. The department is responsible for all sectors of education and learning across all ages.

In Scotland, immediately after devolution, responsibility for policy for lifelong learning was given to a new Department within the Executive, the Enterprise and Lifelong Learning Department, in an attempt to develop a holistic policy for economic development. School education and other services for young people were the concern of another Department within the Executive. In 2007, the Scottish Executive was re-structured: the separate departments were abolished and directorates established around key strategic objectives of the Scottish Government in an effort to improve the co-ordination of policy across the Scottish Government. Adult learning is now within the lifelong learning directorate.

In England, each year the Government sets out its priorities for adult learning through grant letters to the chairs of the Funding Councils. Each Council then allocates and manages funds to achieve the objectives, and a provider's funding will depend on ensuring that the provision they plan and deliver support them. Which courses and students are eligible for state funding, which priority groups are entitled to subsidised provision and what levels of qualification attract funding are thus decided centrally. Provisional plans for new Skills Funding Agency are that it should be less involved in policymaking, and a "light touch" body responsible only for ensuring that public funding is routed swiftly, with an operational remit of implementing the policy decisions made by Ministers.[51]

1.1.4 How are the policy and implementation strategies aligned in England?

A key element of the current Government structure is the attempt to coordinate across Departments, through three key processes:

- a three yearly Comprehensive Spending Review, which examines all areas of Government expenditure every three years, with the aim to allocate resources more directly in response to current Government priorities, rather than on a purely historical basis. The Review then sets Government expenditure plans for the next three years (ensuring greater continuity and predictability than in the past when annual budgeting was used).
- an overarching set of Public Service Agreements (PSAs) which set the major objectives for Government policy. Currently there are 30 of these, which set the framework in which all Government policy is designed and monitored, through associated performance indicators and targets. Each is the responsibility of a lead Department, but all Departments are expected to contribute to achieving all relevant ones. Although only 3 of the PSA targets are owned by DIUS, at least 12 have implications for ALE.
- a regular performance review of Departments against their agreed annual targets, carried out by the Treasury.

---

51 DIUS and DCSF (2008) *Raising Expectations: enabling the system to deliver*, http://www.dcsf.gov.uk/consultations/downloadableDocs/Raising%20Expectations%20pdf.pdf

Policies in other sectors

Neighbourhood renewal and cohesive communities

In January 2001, the Prime Minister launched a national strategy for neighbourhood renewal, with the aim of narrowing the gap between the most deprived neighbourhoods and the rest of the country, so that within 10 to 20 years no one should be seriously disadvantaged by where they live. As well as improving existing services in deprived areas, a number of initiatives were introduced to support and stimulate change. These included a £900m Neighbourhood Renewal Fund; New Deal for Communities partnerships investing around £2 billion over 10 years in 39 of the poorest neighbourhoods; support for community groups; a neighbourhood wardens programme; neighbourhood management schemes; and a skills and knowledge programme to provide training, advice and networking opportunities, and to promote good practice. Also, part of the strategy was the Learning Curve, a 23-point action plan that targets everyone working to transform England's poorest areas, from residents to local and central government.

In a related initiative, the Department for Communities and Local Government is leading a series of policies to build more inclusive and cohesive communities. The particular impact of learning on social cohesion is being explored through ongoing consultations about the role Further and Higher Education providers have on fostering shared values and preventing violent extremism (although mainly focused on young people).[52] In addition, Government has given special attention to courses of English for Speakers of Other Languages (ESOL) in relation to community cohesion. The Government recognises that good English language skills are vital for the integration and social cohesion of communities. Between 2001 and 2004, ESOL spending tripled, reaching just under £300m, partly as a result of the large inflow of immigrants from Eastern Europe following the expansion of the European Union. However an overwhelming demand still outstrips current ESOL supply and DIUS is consulting on the best way to target public funding on the most disadvantaged learners and towards provision that directly fosters community cohesion and integration.

Welfare to Work

As part of its Welfare to Work strategy and as a means of reducing poverty, the Government also introduced a range of New Deal initiatives to help unemployed people across England and Wales into work by closing the gap between the skills employers want and the skills people can offer. The service is tailored to the needs of individuals, supporting them while they prepare for work and find a job, and delivering skills and training that are relevant to local jobs. Since its start, New Deal has helped over 600,000 people to find work. New Deals are aimed particularly at young unemployed people aged 18–24, but other elements are focused on older adults including unemployed people aged 25+ and people aged 50+. There are also

52 DIUS (2008) Promoting good campus relations, fostering shared values and preventing violent extremism in Universities and Higher Education Colleges, http://www.dius.gov.uk/publications/extremismhe.pdf
DIUS (2008) The Role of Further Education Providers in Promoting Community Cohesion, Fostering Shared Values and Preventing Violent Extremism, http://www.dfes.gov.uk/consultations/downloadableDocs/Community%20 Cohesion%20PDF.pdf

specific programmes for lone parents, partners of unemployed people and people with disabilities.

Inter-departmental cooperation to integrate employment and adult skills' initiatives has been developing throughout the decade. Cooperation has been a particular priority because labour market forecasts suggest that there is likely to be significantly fewer job opportunities for those with low levels of skills, and hence increasing social exclusion for them. It is also driven by an underlying view that employment is the most important tool to overcome social exclusion, and give individuals independence and a stake in society. Although unemployment rates are relatively low, a high proportion of people, particularly those over 50, are in receipt of Incapacity Benefit, having been certified unfit for their previous employment. The current policy is to shift from a negative "incapacity" approach, to a positive "capacity" one, concentrating on identifying what people can do, and building skills and confidence to take this on. The shift is part of Government's overarching aspiration to unlock the talent of all British citizens as an imperative to improve social wellbeing and economic competitiveness.

There is a particular concern that many adults who move into work from unemployment return to it relatively quickly or remain in low paid jobs that do not lift them and their families out of poverty. The heart of the new approach to achieve full employment (moving to an 80 per cent employment rate) is to identify the barriers to sustainable employment and progression, and organise welfare and skill systems around tackling them. While in the past, separate targets between the Departments responsible for education and work in England and Wales have led to conflicting initiatives; joint policymaking is now aligning efforts. The Government is now supporting benefit claimants through more intensive and flexible support from a personal adviser, who has discretion to support individuals staying in training, rather than immediately accepting the first job offered, if this is more likely to result in sustainable employment.

Equality and discrimination

The UK has had long standing legislation to outlaw discrimination on grounds of gender, race and disability, with national agencies with remits to challenge discrimination and support change in policies and practice (as well as to support legal challenges to discriminatory practices). More recently, discrimination legislation has been introduced outlawing discrimination on grounds of age, sexual orientation and religion, and support in all six areas has been unified under a new Commission for Equality and Human Rights (CEHR), with a remit to ensure fair treatment; celebrate difference; foster good relations; and to support human rights. All educational institutions are expected to conform to the law, and to actively support anti-discriminatory practice.

During 2009 Government plans to introduce a Single Equality Bill, which will bring together all discrimination law (currently there are over 90 separate legislative documents on discrimination), and establish a universal right to equal treatment.

All statutory education providers are bound by a Single Equality Duty, to promote equality, and publish schemes, which explain their intentions, how performance is to be measured and how complaints will be handled. In Higher Education, an Equality Challenge Unit has been established to support and advise universities in implementing effective equality practices and disseminating examples of excellent practice in relation to both students and staff.

Offender learning and skills

Offenders are much more likely to have poor basic skills needs than the general population, and support for dyslexia and other learning difficulties is a particular problem for practitioners working with offender learners. Historically, education and training for offenders was funded and delivered by the Prison Service (though often contracted out to Further Education Colleges), and involved workshops, industries and some vocational training. This was complemented by basic skills, key skills and support for offenders with learning difficulties and disabilities.

The government's 2001 manifesto included a commitment to 'dramatically improve the quality and quantity of prison education'. Responsibility for delivering this commitment was established in a strategic partnership between the Department for Education and Skills (DfES) and the Prison Service, supported by a new Prisoners Learning and Skills Unit accountable to both DfES and Home Office Ministers.

The creation in 2004 of the National Offender Management Service (NOMS) enabled a more integrated approach to offender learning and skills and responsibility for delivery was placed with the Learning and Skills Council (LSC).

The new Offenders' Learning and Skills Service (OLASS) became fully operational from August 2006 and learning and skills provision has been linked more explicitly with mainstream provision for post-16 learners.[53]

By integrating offender education within mainstream academic and vocational provision and ensuring that offenders experience seamless provision in both custodial and community settings, the LSC hopes to contribute to breaking the cycle of failure that drives re-offending, and reduce the re-offending rate by ten per cent by 2010.

OLASS provides learning and skills in both custody and community settings to prisons, probation services and community, both directly with its contracted providers and through sub-contracting arrangements with other providers including further education colleges, third sector and private training organisations. Other education and training takes place within prisons, probation services and community, which is out of LSC scope and contracting arrangements. Within OLASS, delivery to the 124 public sector prisons in England is contracted to 19 providers, mainly further education colleges, with one Adult Education Service and a small number of private training providers. Additionally, the 9 private sector prisons in England have their own education and training provision and also sub-contract to a variety of providers.

In 2007 the LSC published its "OLASS Prospectus" – a vision for the future delivery of offender learning and skills. The Prospectus aims to:

---

53 In Wales, such responsibilities are to be transferred to the Welsh Assembly Government.

- develop and further reform the way in which learning in custody is planned, organised, delivered and funded – representing a shift away from historical arrangements by prioritising and organising provision according to sentence length, age, type of establishment etc.;[54]
- Widen the scope, range and availability of learning provision for offenders in the community;
- For all offenders, ensure that the learning offer is explicitly linked and aligned to other services and interventions;
- Ensure that all offenders are able to benefit from existing provision and developments within the wider post-16 sector;

Finally, offenders within secure mental health institutions and the Armed Forces Military Corrective Training Centre have their own arrangements for learning and skills, primarily funded by NHS and the MOD.

1.1.5 The main development challenges

In the UK many developmental problems such as exclusion, poverty and discrimination are heavily concentrated in specific locations or groups rather than through larger and general populations. Therefore the main challenge has been targeting policies to reach those farthest away from the labour market and more general social engagement. In this sense, ALE policy has shifted progressively from widening participation, with the aim of increasing the range of people participating, to deepening participation, concentrating resources on more substantial programmes for those in most need, and particularly in securing the skills required for employment.

1.2 Financing of ALE

Adult learning in the UK is funded from a wide variety of public, private and voluntary sources. The national *Inquiry into the Future of Lifelong Learning* is attempting to measure the total scale of this expenditure. Its current work suggests that total expenditure from public sources exceeds £30 billion p.a., while the National Employers Skills Survey suggests that employers spend £38 billion per year. Of this total expenditure, some 95 per cent is spent on learning with an economic purpose.[55]

The scale of voluntary sector expenditure is more difficult to establish. Such assessments are methodologically complex, with major issues about the treatment of employee time for training, about informal workplace training, about training costs embedded in the everyday

---

54 Presentation by Jon Gamble, Director of for Adults and Lifelong Learning, LSC – 8 May 2008 "OLASS the National Context"

55 Government regards all vocational training, basic skills and higher education as being primarily justified in terms of the economic benefits, and the social inclusions benefits which derive from engaging people in rewarding and productive employment.

work of staff in the health and armed services; and about the salary costs of staff employed in training roles within employing organisations. Overall, one might estimate, very roughly, that average expenditure, from all sources, on the education of adults amounts to some £2,000 per head per year.[56] Within this total, levels of expenditure in different kinds of institution, different programmes, and on different kinds of learner, of course, vary greatly.

Government funding is channelled through a set of Funding Councils, which operate at arms length from Government, although their members are appointed by Government, and they are required to response to an annual "letter of guidance" from Government on priorities and approaches.

1.2.1 Public investment in ALE:

Share of the budget allocated to adult education within the education sector

The last decade has seen a very substantial increase in education expenditure in the UK. Over the decade from 1995–6 to 2005–6 total expenditure by the education departments increased in real terms (adjusted for inflation) by 46 per cent, to a total of £67.1 billion (a rise from 4.9 per cent to 5.5 per cent of GDP), of which 29 per cent is spent on post-compulsory education and training

However, the majority of this 29 per cent is spent on the initial education of young people (16–19 year olds in Further Education and 18–22 year olds in Higher Education), and it is not possible to distinguish this from expenditure on adults, since much teaching is in age mixed classes and institutions.

In post-school education and training funding has been strongly targeted on three key policy areas:

- improving basic skills,
- upgrading vocational qualification levels,
- increasing and widening participation in higher education.

In each of these areas there has been significant increase in expenditure on direct provision and on funding of infrastructure, research and development. Figure 3 illustrates the current distribution of public spending on adult learning by the Learning and Skills Council (which is responsible for all funding below higher education level).[57]

Future finance plans are to allocate an increasing share of the budgets through the employer led *Train to Gain* programme, and *Learner Accounts*. Figure 4 illustrates planned public investment for the next four years:

56 Brown, Nigel, Mark Corney and Mick Fletcher (2008) *Study into the Level of Public Investment in Adult Learning*, NIACE.
57 The category of *Adult Learner Responsive* includes the budget for 19+ Further Education, UfI/learndirect and Employability learning. The category of *Employer Responsive* includes the budget for Employer based NVQs, Apprenticeships, work based learning and Train to Gain.

Figure 3 English adult learning public spending 2007–08 in £ million

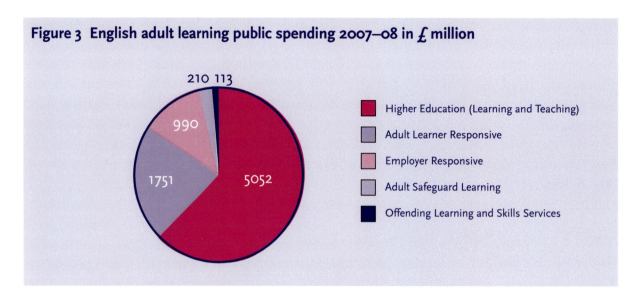

Figure 4 English LSC adult education budget 2007–2010 (thousands £)

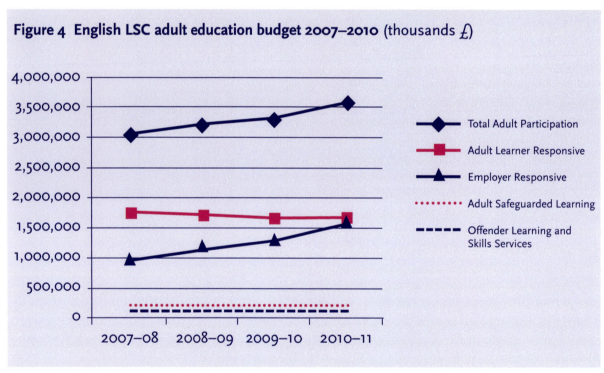

Share of the budget allocated to adult education from other sectors

Other Departments of Government spend money on the education of adults in two ways: in education for the general public or service users (generally related to specific policy objectives, like improving public health), and on training of staff.

The largest investment is in staff training, especially in Health and Social Care, with over 2 million publicly employed staff, and the armed services, where a large proportion of staff time is devoted to training. Current estimates suggest that each spends over £4 billion pa on training.

In more general education, the Ministry of Justice invests in education related to citizenship and social cohesion (including ESOL for refugees and migrants). The Regional Development Agencies spend £600 million p.a. on training for small businesses. Other Departments, including Local Government, Transport, Environment, Food and Rural Affairs, spend smaller sums.

ALE in decentralised/local budgets (local governments and authorities, municipalities, communities);

Although Local Authorities are significant providers of adult education, through their adult education services, the large majority of the funding for such work comes from central Government grants via the Learning and Skills Council, although some adult education is also provided through Local Authority Departments of Leisure and Recreation, or through Departments concerned with economic and social regeneration. This provision is difficult to measure (since the boundaries between activities and learning are not easily defined) and the total sums have never been quantified.

Other investment

International funding does not play a large part in adult education in the UK. The exception has been the European Social Fund (ESF), which has provided match funding to a large number of experimental projects and programmes, especially directed at overcoming social exclusion, and concentrated in areas of economic restructuring.

1.2.2 Foreign bilateral/multilateral donor investment in ALE:

The UK does not receive significant sums of this kind for adult learning.

1.2.3 Support to ALE from private/corporate sector:

It is difficult to produce reliable data on employer expenditure on education for adults. The National Employer Skills Survey suggests (on the basis of self reporting by a very large sample of employers) that employers spend some £38.6 billion per year on training (including the costs of lost staff time, which accounts for the majority of the costs). This is larger that the total sum spent by public agencies on general education (Further, Higher, and Adult) and on training their own staff, estimated in a recent study as around £31 billion per year.[58]

Research suggests that a high proportion of employer expenditure is devoted to induction of new employees and mandatory training required to comply with law, especially relation to health and safety. Beyond this, employer funded training tends to be concentrated on those in higher status jobs, who tend also to be those employees with the most previous education and training. The level of investment varies very greatly between employing organisations, by size, sector and history. A particular problem is costing of informal workplace training, where recent research (see 3.1 below) suggests that much of the most important learning which

58 Unpublished study for the National Inquiry into the Future of Lifelong Learning

employees do is undertaken informally with colleagues in the workplace, and not separately recorded or accounted for as "training".

A report on the UK employer training market in 2005–6 produced by MarketResearch.com, found the market broadly static, with some pockets of growth. It suggested that 'the key reasons appear to be that profitability in many of the UK's companies is severely under pressure and fee rates in the training sector are being reduced. The other reason was that the training sector was still struggling to make the economic case for training and development'. The report forecasted that, between 2006/2007 and 2010/2011, the UK training market, as measured by employer expenditure on off-the-job training, would experience modest growth, rising by 1 per cent per year. It further reported that demand for training was challenged by a lack of time and resources, and that 'short courses have become popular, with an increase in "bite-size"[59] learning'. Demand for E-learning had proved to be lower than expected, though this delivery mode had by no means disappeared. Finally the report suggested a trend towards courses with an 'obvious clear-cut benefit'. An example cited was courses concerned with how to comply with new legislation; with less demand for courses in generic skills and areas such as diversity training and emotional intelligence.

1.2.4 Civil society support to ALE

There are a small number of voluntary agencies which are significant providers of general education for adults. These include the Workers Educational Association, the National Federation of Women's' Institutes, and the University of the Third Age. The first two receive some public funding to support their work; the third operates a largely voluntary model of education where members teach each other on an unpaid basis.

In addition, a very large range of voluntary agencies provide some form of education to the general public about their particular field of interest, and to the volunteers and paid staff who work for them. The voluntary sector in the UK is very large and complex (it has been estimated that there are over half a million organisations), and the extent of the educational provision has never been systematically measured, partly because so much is embedded in the everyday workings of the organisations where it is difficult to define and track

A major contribution to informal learning comes from broadcasters, and especially the BBC, which has public education as a key element of its Charter. In addition to broadcasting documentary and current affairs programmes, broadcasters produce a range of programmes aiming to develop skills in fields like cookery and gardening and appreciation of the arts, theatre and music. Such programmes are often accompanied by books, websites and other support materials to encourage viewers to pursue the subject further, or to join some sort of formal class. Occasionally the BBC organises a major educational initiative. An example is the recent "People's War" project, in which broadcasts about the Second World War (covering political, military, and social perspectives) were accompanied by extensive websites, with discussion forums. A major objective was to encourage individuals to submit accounts of their personal experiences of life during the war, creating a very large publicly accessible archive.

---

59 "bite size training" is training delivered in very small pieces, usually aimed at very specific skills.

Similar initiatives are provided by museums and libraries, where public admission charges were abolished early in the decade, resulting in an increase of over 60 per cent in attendances in 2002.

Another important agency is the National Institute of Adult Continuing Education (NIACE), an independent non-governmental organisation and charity whose purpose is to supports adult learning, through policy work, research, publications and conferences. Its corporate and individual members come from a range of places where adults learn: in further education colleges and local community settings; in universities, workplaces and prisons. Its aim is to secure more, different and better opportunities for adult learners, in both formal and informal settings, and with a particular concern for the interests of those who have benefited least from education and training in UK society.

1.2.5 Learners'/individuals' contributions to ALE

Government policy is that, over time, the proportion of the costs of ALE paid by individuals should increase, with the state's contribution not being reduced, but being increasingly focused on specific areas of market failure. Thus the state guarantees free provision for all those studying for basic skills/Skills for Life qualifications, and for their first Level 2 qualification. It also prioritises courses leading to full qualifications, rather than short courses or modules. However, for many other areas of adult education (notably those aimed at cultural, social and non-vocational purposes) learners have always been expected to pay fees covering a significant proportion of the full cost, and this proportion has been rising as policy has focused more sharply on the key priority groups and subjects.

The broad policy of shifting the balance of payment between the state, individual and employer also applies in higher education, where student tuition fees were introduced for the first time for young undergraduates in 1998. The maximum level of fee is limited to £3,149 p.a. (2008/9), and Universities are only able to charge such fees if they satisfy a Regulator, the Office of Fair Access, that they are making appropriate arrangements to secure wider participation from underrepresented groups. A complex arrangement of student loans and bursaries provided by Universities to poorer students is aimed at ensuring that poorer students are not prevented from participation.

This broad policy has had positive effects. The numbers of students on prioritised programmes, and the numbers achieving qualifications have risen. However, it has also had the unintended effect of suddenly raising student fees for short courses and courses not linked to recognised qualifications, which has led to a substantial drop in enrolments on such programmes in both Further and Higher Education. In Further Education total numbers of students have fallen, while the numbers on long, and qualification bearing, courses has risen. In Higher Education there has not been a dramatic increase in the numbers of under-graduates from disadvantaged backgrounds. Recent research suggests that most of those who have the required entry qualifications for higher education (whatever their background) do in fact enter, and that the problem lies in ensuring that disadvantaged young people succeed in school. Over the decade there has, however, been a progressive decline in the numbers of higher education students on non qualification-bearing courses.

In 2000, the Scottish Executive decided to abolish pre-paid tuition fees for Scottish students at Scottish universities. However Scottish students did have to pay a "graduate endowment" which went into a student hardship fund. In February 2008 Members of the Scottish Parliament voted to abolish this charge, which was, by then, £2,289.

After initially deciding not to impose higher education tuition fees in Wales, the Welsh Assembly Government decided in 2005 to allow its universities to charge students tuition fees of up to £3,000, but students living in Wales would only pay £1,200 and the Assembly Government would contribute the balance. Students from other parts of the UK in Welsh institutions would pay the full £3,000 and Welsh students who studied in colleges outside of Wales would also be liable to pay £3,000, except for courses like veterinary science which are not available in Welsh Universities.

Northern Ireland Ministers are currently consulting on legislation to introduce a similar arrangement to those in place for England.

1.2.6 Financial incentives in support of ALE

For some years there has been interest in ways of making adult education provision more responsive to "customer" demand, and this is now an established plank of Government policy. One tool for this is the creation of a system of learner accounts, funded, or partly funded by the State, which would put purchasing power for ALE (or some forms of it) in the hands of individuals.

This approach was first tried in 2000 with a scheme of Individual Learning Accounts, in which individuals could claim up to £150 if they invested £25 or their own money in a virtual "account". They could then use the total sum to buy vocational courses of specified types. The scheme was very successful in stimulating participation, and 2.5 million people took up accounts over the 14-month period that the scheme operated. Unfortunately its success created unsustainable pressure on available funds, and on administrative and auditing systems, and the scheme was closed in England and Scotland (although schemes continued in Wales and in the National Health Service). Scotland has now introduced a modified individual ILA targeted on those with lower incomes and also offering support for those on low incomes on part-time HE courses. A new scheme Adult Learner Accounts is now being piloted on a small scale in two English Regions in the 2007–8 academic year, with accounts only available for learning at Level 3.

Learning lessons from ILAs and the ALA trials, and in response to a recommendation of the Leitch Report, a new and ambitious universal Skills Account is being developed for launch in England from 2010, (with pilots beginning in September 2008 in two Regions). Skills Accounts will be virtual accounts giving individuals a "voucher" setting out the notional value of state funding towards a course. This will represent an entitlement which can be spent at an accredited learning provider of their choice as full or part contribution towards a course. Skills Accounts holders will be able to access their personal account online, and see a verified record of their qualifications, attached to their Unique Learner Number, as well as the investment that has been made in their learning over a lifetime.

A clear risk in such a "customer driven" approach is that individuals will be ill informed about the opportunities available, and their relevance to their personal circumstances and aspirations. To counter this, a new universal adult advancement and careers service will also be in place from 2010 to ensure that individuals are able to make well informed decisions on the use of the Skills Accounts.

A variety of other financial support mechanisms exist. They include the Adult Learning Grant which pays up to £30 per week to support adults on low incomes studying full-time towards a first Level 2 or Level 3 qualification Learners, who must be studying at a Learning and Skills Council funded learning provider may use their grant to meet costs of travel, childcare, study materials, etc.

A different mechanism is the Career Development Loan. This is a deferred repayment bank loan arranged between the individual and participating high street banks (with similar mechanisms in Scotland and Wales).

One clear risk in such an approach is that "customers" may be ill informed about the opportunities available, and may make "unwise" purchasing decisions. One way of limiting this risk is the development of good information and advice systems, which is being addressed through the creation in England of a new inclusive Adult Advancement and Careers Service.

A variety of other financial support mechanisms exist. They include the Adult Learning Grant which pays up to £30 per week to support adults on low incomes studying full-time towards a first Level 2 or Level 3 qualification in an approved further education college. The allowance is meant to help towards covering the costs of travel, study materials, etc.

A different mechanism is the Career Development Loan, a personal loan arranged between the LSC and high street banks (with similar mechanisms in Scotland). This allows the individual to borrow anything between £300 and £8,000 to help fund up to two years of learning in a wide variety of eligible courses. The money can be used to pay the course fees but it can also be used to cover other course costs like, childcare, travel, books and equipment or for living expenses. The LSC pays the loan interest while the individual is learning, and for one month after completion, after which the individual repays the loan to the bank over an agreed period at a fixed rate of interest.

For those participating in higher education there is a complex system of financial support. Full time students are eligible for income contingent student loans to cover tuition fees and accommodation costs (in total up to £9,620) repayable only when the graduate is earning over £15,000 p.a. There are also means tested grants for accommodation costs of up to £2,835. Individual institutions also offer bursaries to particular kinds of students, and some offer scholarships based on income or academic performance.

1.2.7 Benchmarks (targets) in relation to financing of ALE

There is no benchmarking of finance for ALE. The UK Government view is that benchmarking should be done on the basis of outcomes rather than inputs.

2 Quality: provision, participation and achievement

2.1 Provision of ALE and institutional frameworks

2.1.1 Institutions responsible for managing and co-ordinating ALE at national level

The largest body of adult learning provision is made through Further Education Colleges and Universities.[60] All are constitutionally independent of Government, although all are heavily dependent on Government funding through the relevant Funding Councils, and their priorities are heavily influenced by Government through the Councils.

In England there are 378 Further Education Colleges, which deliver general education, initial vocational education and continuing professional development to people post-16 (the minimum school leaving age). Together they provide for some 2.4 million learners each year, of whom two thirds are over 19 at the point of entry.

There are 168 higher education institutions[61] providing first and postgraduate degrees, Foundation Degrees, and non-accredited programmes. They provide for 2.4 million learners, of whom over half are over 19 at entry (52 per cent of first year undergraduates).

In England the large majority of Government funding for ALE is channelled through the two large Funding Councils – the Higher Education Funding Council, with an annual budget for teaching at degree level of £4.7 billion and the Learning and Skills Council, with an annual adult budget of £3.1 billion for work which is mainly below first degree level. The Councils are formally autonomous, although their members are appointed by the Government, they operate within a budget set by central Government, and they are expected to take note of an annual grant letter of guidance from the relevant Secretary of State. During the last decade, these letters have become increasingly prescriptive about priorities and which programmes and activities are to be funded.

A major and distinctive, feature of UK ALE has been its strong publicly funded "non-vocational" adult education service. This was provided through Local Authorities until the creation of the Learning and Skills Council in 2001, when the funds were incorporated into the overall budget of the LSC in England and the National Council for Education and Training for Wales (ELWa) for Wales. Prior to that point Local Authorities had discretion over how

---

60 Including other institutions of Higher Education which do not formally call themselves Universities.
61 132 in England, 13 in Scotland, 12 in Wales and 2 in Northern Ireland. 106 are Universities, and 62 are other institutions (specialist Colleges etc).

much to spend on such services, and levels of provision varied from almost nothing, to extensive sets of large adult education colleges with large programmes involving thousands of learners. When the budget was transferred to the LSC, Government guaranteed that a sum equal to that previously spent by Local Authorities (£210 million p.a.) would be protected for similar provision (and the provision came to be known as "safeguarded" adult education for that reason).

There are no separate adult education centres or institutes in Northern Ireland, where adult education courses (including academic, vocational and leisure courses) are provided by the 16 colleges which comprise the statutory further education sector. In Scotland funding from the Scottish government is passed to the 32 local authorities to Community Learning Strategy Partnerships where local providers of adult learning have access to resources. Strategic plans are submitted by all partnerships, which indicate how the funding will be used to build capacity and a wide range of learning opportunities across all sectors.

2.1.2 Summary of the ALE programmes in the UK

The main programmes are listed in the table at Annex 1.

2.1.3 Linkages between formal and non-formal approaches

The creation of linkages and progression routes between different parts of post-school education has been a theme of UK education policy since the 1980s. Key elements of this have been ongoing work to create a national qualification and credit framework described below. This was also part of the driving force for the creation of the comprehensive national framework of outcome based National Vocational Qualifications, and of Foundation degrees, both of which aim to help bridge the academic vocational divide. However, two other initiatives are mentioned below.

Two particular structures exist to improve linkages between formal and non-formal learning: Open College Networks and Access Courses.

Open Colleges Network

The Open College Network (OCN) movement was created in the 1980s by local networks of providers who collaborated in order to negotiate agreements on equivalences between qualifications, especially focusing on the outcomes of non-formal and informal education at local level. These local consortia now cover most of the UK, and have formed a National Open College Network (which celebrated its 20th anniversary in 2007), which coordinates and supports their work, and represents them in the negotiations over the new Qualifications and Credit Framework.

Local OCNs involve a wide range of providers, from local community groups and employer training providers to Universities. They provide quality assurance for learning programmes, moderate and verify learner achievement and award certificates. They also provide advice to local providers and a database of approved units of accreditation. At the core of the OCN process is the collaborative scrutinising of curricula and assessment processes to allocate level, volume and credit value to individual locally devised programmes. Learners are given a record or passport in which credits awarded by the OCN are recorded, and can be used to build towards formal qualification and progression.

Access courses

In response to widespread concern in the 1980s that traditional school based qualifications used for higher education entry might be inappropriate for mature applicants, an Access Course movement emerged, led by adult educators. This developed special courses designed for adult learners, usually placing special emphasis on using learners' life experience, and organised in more flexible ways than the traditional programmes. These are now formally recognised as an alternative route into higher education for mature learners. Courses are validated by local Authorised Validating Agencies (24 in England and Wales in 2005) approved by QAA, and some of these are also OCNs. In 2005 there were 1,200 Access courses in England and Wales, with the following the most popular subjects:

Table 3 Most popular Access course subjects

Subject	Percentage of courses
General studies	17
Medicine related	16
Social studies	11
Creative arts	9
Education	7
Combined science	6
Maths and computer science	6
Business and administration	5

2.1.4 Certification and national awards

Qualifications and Credit Frameworks

Historically in the UK, academic (school level), vocational and higher education qualifications were all organised and managed separately, and there was no direct agreed equivalence between them. In the 1980s, concern to make transition between the different systems easier and more flexible led to the development of a broad agreement to define all qualifications in terms of level and volume. This was used to facilitate transitions, and contributed to some growth in arrangements to accredit prior learning (APL) and prior experiential learning (APEL). At the same time there was a general overhaul of vocational qualifications, to create the framework of National Vocational Qualifications, each of which is specified in outcomes terms and assigned to a level in a national framework.

In Scotland, the Scottish Credit and Qualifications Framework was formally launched in 2001, and provided a comprehensive framework including HE and academic and vocational qualifications, and clarifies the relationship between qualifications and routes for progression, and improves recognition of learners achievements. It continues to be modified to include all forms of learning and develop links with other frameworks.

Efforts to harmonise the separate systems across the UK through a Qualifications Framework have been in progress since the mid 1990s, and a major consolidation was begun in 2004 to create a new Qualifications and Credit Framework (QCF) which is currently intended to incorporate post-19 vocational qualifications (excluding higher education qualifications) in England, Wales and Northern Ireland, described in unit and credit terms. This will include employers' qualifications where the employer has been formally recognised as an awarding organisation. It is likely that the QCF will be extended to include general qualifications and qualifications for 14–19 year olds (fully replacing the existing National Qualification Framework), and it has been designed to enable this. The QCF will allow greater flexibility in the structure of qualifications thanks to the unit structure, and consistent titles regarding size, level and content of qualifications will allow learners and employers to identify appropriate qualifications more easily. Scotland already has an established credit framework – the Scottish Credit and Qualifications Framework which makes better links between qualifications and improves recognition of learners' achievements. The Scottish Framework will use a similar structure, but remain independent, placing more emphasis on whole qualifications, rather than units of them. All Sector Skills Councils have been involved in the development of vocational qualifications within this framework, and the LSC is currently studying the feasibility of using units as a basis for funding colleges. The intention is that by the end of 2010 all post-19 vocational qualifications will have migrated from the NQF into the QCF.

The new framework has eight levels, and Figure 5, taken from the Welsh Skills Strategy, shows how these are structured. It illustrates, with examples, the levels of qualifications and the relevant learning provision.

Figure 5 Credits and Qualifications Framework for Wales: Learning and Progression Routes

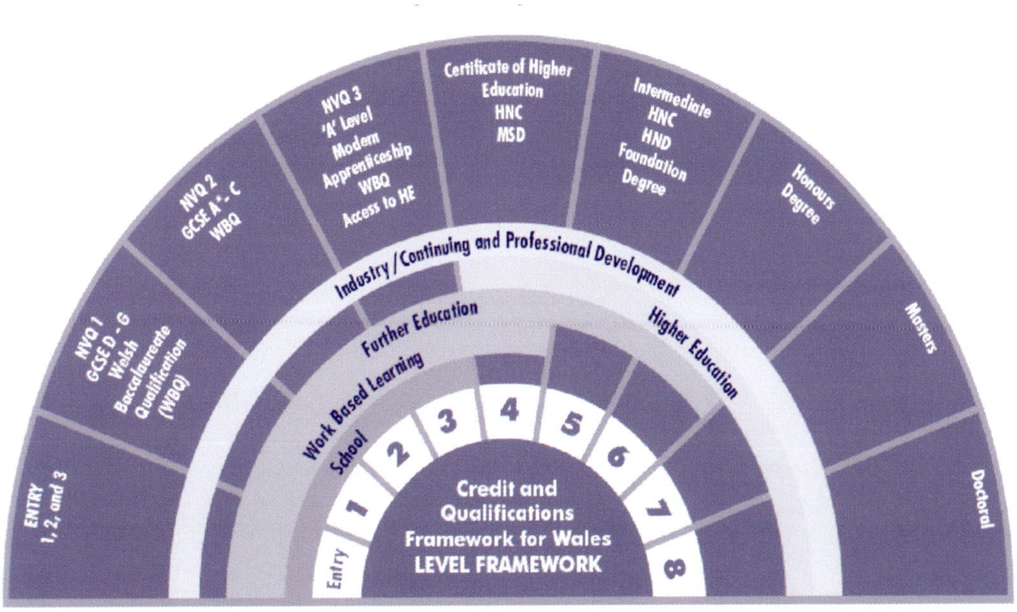

2.2 Participation in ALE

2.2.1 Statistical data on participation

The UK has a continuing challenge to increase participation in learning, especially among those who are most hard to reach and the most resistant "non-learners".[62] Over recent years, increasing efforts have been made to measure adult participation in learning in the UK, partly as a result of the establishment of education targets. However, outside provision directly funded by the Education Departments and their agencies, determining an exact measure of participation is difficult as it is strongly influenced by the methodology and definition of learning used, the age cohort surveyed[63] and the willingness of providers to provide data.

The UK has several surveys on adult learning participation rates, of which five are particularly relevant:

- The Government's *Annual Population Survey* (linked to the Labour Force Survey) uses a broad definition of learning but is only for England;
- The annual NIACE *Adult Learning Survey* also uses a broad definition and includes the entire UK population;
- The LSC's *Statistical First Release* includes much more detailed information about individual learners, but only on formal courses funded by the LSC itself in England;
- The Government's *National Adult Learner Survey* (NALS) for England and Wales (Scotland has participated since 2005)
- Higher Education Statistical Agency (HESA) records all participation in award bearing programmes in UK Higher Education Institutions but does not include the substantial volume of short non-award bearing courses (both for employers and for the general public)

Between 1997 and 2001, total enrolments in English publicly funded programmes below higher education level rose significantly, mainly on relatively short courses in Further Education Colleges, encouraged by a funding strategy which encouraged subsidised participation. Since then, policy has encouraged concentration on "deeper", rather than "wider" participation, with fewer learners engaged on longer, mainly qualification bearing, courses, and courses focused on basic skills and specific vocational qualifications. As a result, overall student numbers on formal English LSC funded courses on Further Education Colleges have reduced to below the 1997 level, although the total volume of activity (measured in taught hours) has continued to grow (see Figure 6).[64]

---

62 The term "non-learner" is widely used, although conceptually it is misleading – very few (if any) people do not learn, though many choose not to do so in recognisable educational settings.

63 McGivney, V. (2001) *Fixing or changing the pattern: reflections on widening adult participation in learning*, Leicester: NIACE

64 Due to changes in the data collection systems of the Statistical First Release, data for 2003/04 and earlier years is not comparable with later years.

Figure 6 Adult Learners on LSC-funded FE provision 1996–2007 (England)

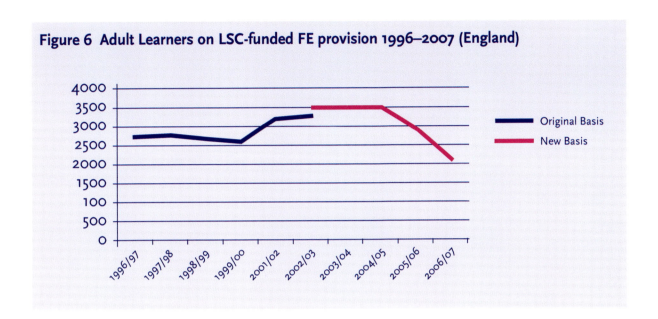

Looking at broad definitions of adult learning, the Government's *Annual Population Survey*[65] (APS) measures people aged 16 to 69 in England participating in learning of any kind. The most recent report shows that in 2006, 68.2 per cent of all adults reported participating in some type of learning[66] and 46.4 per cent (14.9 million) participated in taught courses.[67] However, between 2002/03 and 2005/06 the numbers participating fell by 2.4 million learners (in any kind of learning) and 4.1 million in taught courses (see Figure 7).

The *Adult Learning Survey* carried out annually by the National Institute of Adult Continuing Education (NIACE),[68] confirms this picture. The survey, which interviews a weighted sample of adults, aged 17 and over, in the UK also uses a broad definition of learning, to include independent learning in the home and workplace over the last three years. These again show a rise from 1996 to 2002, but with a downward trend in total participation over the last two years.

65 DIUS (2007) *Qualifications and Participation in Learning at a local level: England 2006*, http://www.dfes. gov.uk/rsgateway/DB/STA/t000747/addition6ParticipationInLearning.xls
66 Studying for qualifications without taking part in a taught course; supervised training while doing a job; time spent keeping up-to-date with developments in one's work or profession; deliberately trying to improve one's knowledge about anything or teach oneself a skill without taking part in a taught course.
67 Taught courses that were meant to lead to a qualification; taught courses designed to help develop skills used in a job; courses, instructions or tuition in driving, playing a musical instrument, art or craft, sport or any practical skill; evening classes; learning involving an individual working on their own from a package of materials provided by an employer, college, commercial organisation or other training provider, other taught course, instruction or tuition
68 Aldridge, Fiona and Alan Tuckett (2008) *Counting the Costs*, Leicester: NIACE

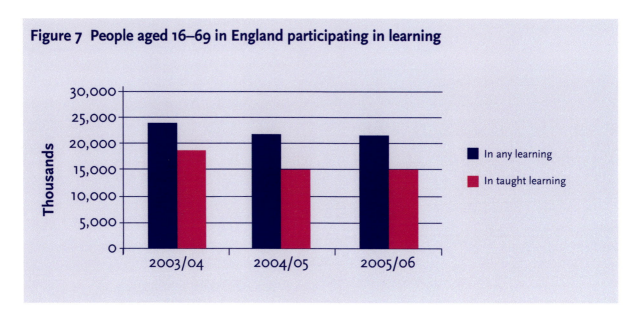

Figure 7 People aged 16–69 in England participating in learning

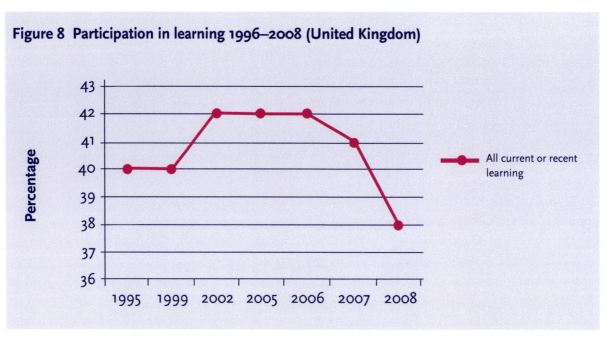

Figure 8 Participation in learning 1996–2008 (United Kingdom)

The LSC's *Statistical First Release*[69] series, produces detailed information on all LSC funded adult (19+) learners in England (adult students in further education, work based learning, *Train to Gain* and Adult Safeguarded Learning). This shows a total of 3.16 million LSC funded learners over 18 in 2006/07, following a drop of 1.38 million over the past three years (a drop of 30.36 per cent) weighted towards older learners. This decline is, however, a result of a deliberate policy to focus Government support on priority groups and subjects, and the effect

69 LSC (2008) *Further Education, Work Based Learning, Train to Gain and Adult Safeguarded Learning – Learner Numbers in England: October 2007*, http://readingroom.lsc.gov.uk/lsc/National/nat-ilrsfr15final-apr08.pdf

of this "deepening" strategy can be seen in figures 9 and 10, which show adult learners on the key LSC priority programmes rising, against the broader trend of a decline of participation in adult learning.

Figure 9 Adult learners in LSC-funded priority programmes in FE colleges

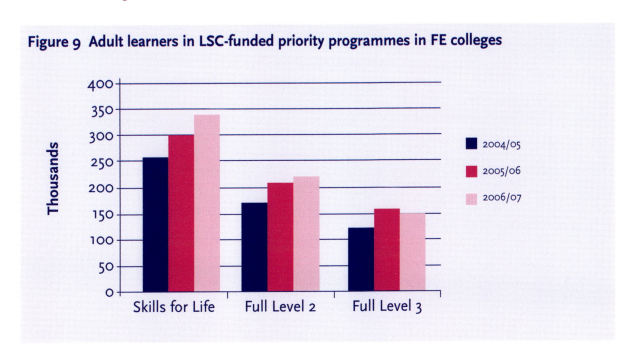

Figure 10 Adult learners in all LSC-funded programmes in FE colleges

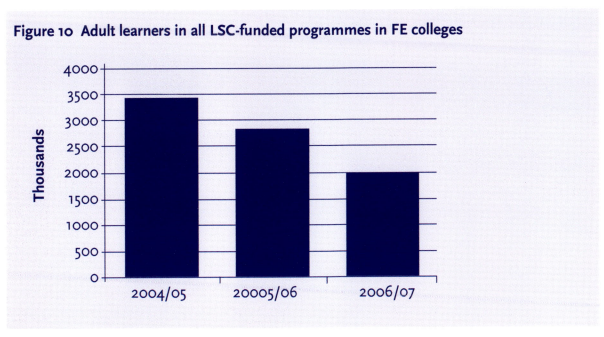

2.2.2 Surveys/studies undertaken on non-participation and difficult to reach groups

The Government's *National Adult Learning Survey*[70] (NALS) series (carried out in 1997, 2001, 2002 and 2005) shows the continuing influence of initial education on later life learning, with adult participation dominated by those with the longest initial education (which in turn tends to correlate with social class and membership of specific minority ethnic groups). Interestingly, the impact of previous education is lowest for those in non-vocational programmes.

Table 4 Percentages of respondents leaving continuous full-time education at different ages reporting different types of learning (England and Wales)

School leaving age	16 or younger	17–18	19–20	21 or older	Total
Any learning	72	85	88	94	80
Taught learning	53	68	73	78	62
Self-directed learning	54	71	71	86	65
Vocational learning	63	78	84	90	73
Non-vocational learning	23	26	27	27	25

NALS 2005

Gender

In terms of absolute numbers, gender is not a major issue in UK adult learning participation. Although there remain issues about what kinds of learning women have access to and on what terms, their overall participation rates are broadly similar to men's, and tend to exceed them in recent years, as the NIACE survey shows.

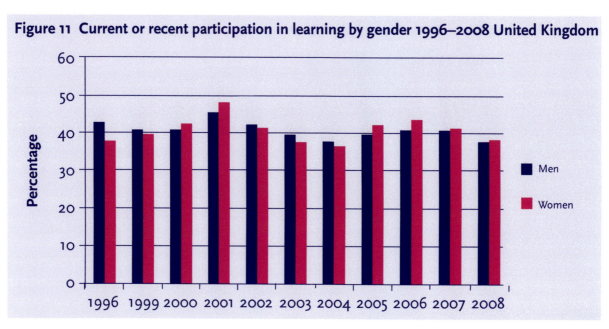

Figure 11 Current or recent participation in learning by gender 1996–2008 United Kingdom

70 Finch, Steven *et al.* (2005) *National Adult Learning Survey 2005*, http://www.dfes.gov.uk/research/data/uploadfiles/RR815.pdf

Ethnicity

Participation rates by different ethnic groups are, however, a continuing issue. As the NIACE 2008 survey[71] shows, when grouped together, members of ethnic minorities were as likely to participate as white adults, but this masks very serious variation between groups. The groups least likely to participate were people of Pakistani and Bangladeshi origin, while people of black African origin, and of mixed origin were the most likely to participate.

Figure 12 Adult participation in learning by ethnicity (United Kingdom)

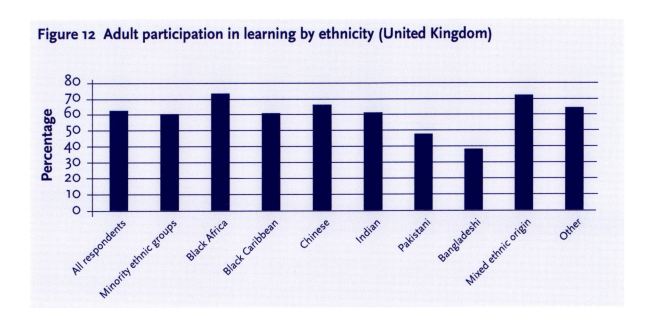

Social class

The NIACE 2008[72] figures show a continuing strong social class bias in participation. Among those participating in current or recent learning 51 per cent belong to the upper and upper-middle classes while only 26 per cent belong to those in semi-skilled and unskilled work, retired people and those dependent upon welfare benefits. Furthermore since 2006 there has been a particularly sharp decline of 7 percentage points among skilled manual workers (class C2) (see Figure 13).

71 Aldridge, Fiona, Hayley Lamb and Alan Tuckett (2008) *Are we closing the gap?*, Leicester : NIACE.
72 Aldridge, Fiona and Alan Tuckett (2008) *Counting the cost*, Leicester: NIACE.

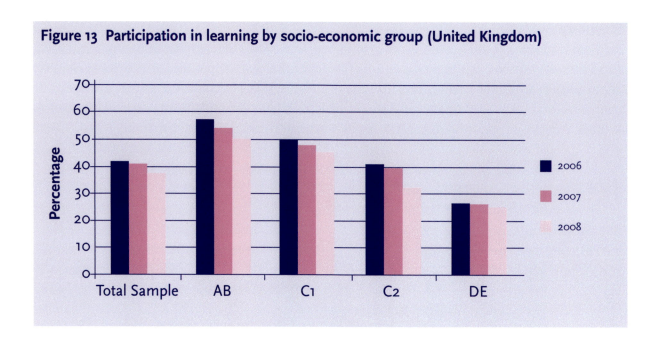

Figure 13 Participation in learning by socio-economic group (United Kingdom)

2.2.3 Surveys/studies of learner motivation

The 2005 NIACE survey asked specific questions about motivation to participate in learning. The results, illustrated in Figure 14, show a mixture of employability and personal responses. There is a predictable shift away from the former as people age. "Improve my self confidence" is cited by fewer than 4 per cent of people 45–54s but by 32 per cent of people 65–74.

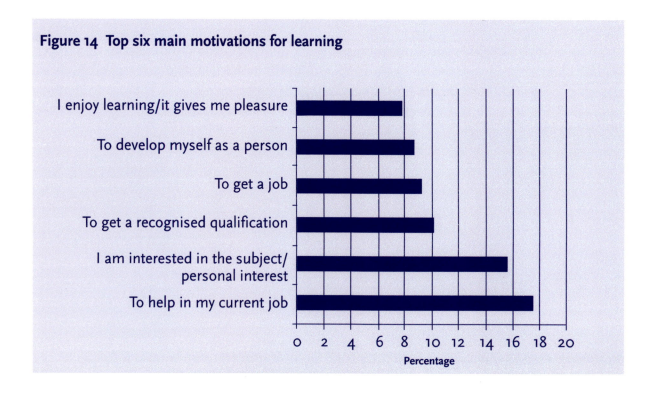

Figure 14 Top six main motivations for learning

The attitudes of learners and non-learners are also analysed in NALS 2005 (table 5 below). While, predictably, the learners are more positive in their attitudes to learning than non-learners, a clear majority of *both* groups see learning as important and fun, and something they are interested in doing, and fewer than 20 pre cent of non-learners feel that "education is not for people like me". However, one in four respondents reported negative experience of school.

Table 5 Attitudes to learning

	Agree Strongly	Agree Slightly	Neither Agree nor	Disagree Slightly	Disagree Strongly
Learning is something you should do throughout your life					
Learner	76	19	4	1	1
Non-learner	57	28	9	4	3
Learning new things is fun					
Learner	50	35	12	2	1
Non-learner	38	41	14	4	2
I'm not interested in doing any learning					
Learner	2	3	6	12	77
Non-learner	19	10	12	19	40
I didn't get anything useful out of school					
Learner	6	8	7	14	63
Non-learner	13	13	8	23	43
Learning isn't for people like me					
Learner	1	2	4	13	80
Non-learner	9	10	14	21	46

2.2.4 Measures to mobilise learners and to increase participation

Get on

Government funds a number of campaigns and activities to stimulate demand for adult learning, and a "duty to promote learning" is included in the remit of the LSC. The Welsh Assembly Government has the same responsibility in Wales. One of the biggest and most successful campaigns is the *Get On* campaign, which formed part of the Government's *Skills for Life* strategy, which aimed to help 2.25 million learners gain a qualification by 2010. In its first stage launched in 2001 it featured a now-famous "gremlin"[73] character in television and press advertising, encouraged people with literacy, numeracy and language needs to tackle their fears or "gremlins" of basic skills.

73 A grotesque unattractive cartoon character, presented as blocking people's access to learning and life progression.

Bite Size

Also in 2001, the Learning and Skills Council launched a nationwide *Bite Size* campaign to attract adults back into learning. Held over four weeks, *Bite Size* was one of the largest adult learning initiatives ever seen in England, attracting learners into some 18,000 short courses, to have a free, "no commitment" taste of learning. This too was linked to a major advertising campaign in the national press and television. Almost a fifth of those taking part in the taster programmes were new learners and a subsequent survey revealed that over 40 per cent had gone on to further learning. A second campaign, featuring a TV celebrity, took place in 2003 when thousands of *Bitesize Intros* (very short "taster" lessons) were available in scores of accessible locations to encourage many more adults back into learning. The objective was to attract 50,000 adult learners, with 25 per cent being new learners who have done little or no learning since leaving school. In total, more than 70,000 learners attended one of over 32,000 Intros held throughout the country with over 85 per cent of learners going on to, or planning to enrol on, further courses. However, this initiative has not subsequently been repeated.

Our future: its in our hands

The most recent marketing campaign to get adults to sign up to learning, *Our future, it's in our hands*, was launched in 2007 and is also led by the LSC. It is the most ambitious communications campaign to date and will run for five years. It seeks to encourage and inspire employers and individuals to take control of their lives by investing in skills. The campaign aims to provide everyone with easy to access information through a dedicated campaign phone line and website that will be a "one-stop shop" for all skills training information and support.

Adult Learners' Week

Government also supports Adult Learners' Week, coordinated by NIACE, which provides an opportunity to celebrate, promote and advance all forms of adult learning. In May 2008 the 17th Adult Learners' Week offered over 5,000 local events, and more than 100 awards for adult learners and organisations. Each year, the winners of the awards are celebrated at national and regional conferences and in the media, and their stories have proved powerful motivators for new learners. They aim to show that learning does not stop with initial schooling and that, with determination, many barriers can be overcome. The Week is backed by a freephone helpline provided by *UfI/Learndirect*, and staffed by adult guidance specialists from all over the UK. The UK Government, the Welsh Assembly Government and the European Social Fund, are keen supporters and core funders of Adult Learners' Week, enabling the co-ordinator, NIACE, to run national events, co-ordinate awards and regional work, and provide small amounts of funding to support local work associated with the Week.[74]

74 See www.vqday.org.uk

2.2.5 Specific groups targeted by ALE provision

The Government's main aim is to upskill the UK population, to increase international competitiveness and to narrow the gap between those with high level qualifications and what has been described as the 'long tail of underachievement'. Historically employers and individuals have not invested in qualifications at Level 2, as there is no immediate measurable benefit in terms of increased productivity, pay or job security. However skills at this level are seen as being an essential platform for future skills development. In order to address this market failure and to help fulfil their aim of creating a high-skill economy, the Government has therefore decided to focus the investment of public education funds in helping people achieve a *Skills for Life* qualification, a full Level 2 qualification or a Level 3 qualification. In parallel, the Department for Work and Pensions funds a wide range of initiatives aimed at enabling unemployed people, including those whose health or disability constrains their employment choices, back into work.

2.2.6 Participation benchmarks

The current benchmarks for education are defined in the cross-Government Public Service Agreements (PSAs), which set targets for all public policy, and to which all Departments are expected to contribute. Three of the PSAs are directly related to post-school education (on skills, early drop out from education, and equality), but at least 9 others have some relevance (see 2.3.4 below and Annex 7). The UK's general approach is to express benchmarks as targets, expressed in terms of outcomes rather than simple participation.

2.3 Monitoring and evaluating programmes and assessing learning outcomes

Quality assurance in education in the UK has passed through a series of radical changes since the early 1990s. In the 1980s Government began a process of centralising an education system which had been highly devolved, flexible and variable in quality. In the mid 1990s, in response to evidence of very variable standards in education at all levels, the incoming Government put in place a rigorous set of quality assurance processes, involving very detailed reporting, and intensive inspection.

The results were used to provide identify "failing" institutions in need of support, and to provide public information, to enable learners to more informed choices between institutions. Over time, inspections and monitoring data showed clear improvement, particularly in the poorest performing institutions, and the ongoing costs of this regime (to institutions and Government) were felt to be disproportionate. As a result, Government has introduced a "lighter touch" approach, in which institutions that have demonstrated their quality are examined less frequently, with attention being increasingly concentrated on the weakest ones. As part of this process, responsibility for quality assurance is being passed gradually to organisations "owned" by the institutions themselves, rather than direct agencies of Government.

Further Education and Higher Education have distinct quality assurance systems and institutions, although the underlying principles are similar in both cases. In Higher Education, quality is overseen by the Quality Assurance Agency for Higher Education (QAA), created in 1997, and owned and managed by the Universities themselves. In Further Education it is the responsibility of the Office for Standards in Education (Ofsted – which is also responsible for quality assurance in schools and children's services).

In both FE and HE the underlying philosophy is of continuous improvement, concentrating attention (inspection, audit and developmental work) on institutions which have not yet demonstrated high quality. The expectation is that, in a mass participation further and higher education system, students, employers and the general public all need clear information to assist them when choosing courses, qualifications and institutions to attend. Heavy emphasis is given to responsiveness to employer needs, since this is seen as critical to economic productivity and social inclusion. A very large volume of performance data is collected and published, from the level of the individual learner to the whole system, and this is used extensively in formulating policy and allocating funding.

Both systems rest on the assessment of defined learning outcomes, and the systematic gathering of data about learners and their achievements against those outcomes. The key difference is that in Higher Education the design and assessment of most programmes are determined by the individual institutions (sometimes in consultation with relevant employers or professional bodies, and with a system of external examiners to oversee assessment), while in Further Education they are generally determined by external Awarding Bodies, who define the content and assessment methods of individual programmes. Both systems have some difficulty in managing quality assurance in relation to learning which does not lead to formal qualifications.

In Wales, *Estyn*, Her Majesty's Inspectorate for Education and Training, undertakes inspection of adult learning in Wales. Estyn's aim is to raise standards and quality in education and training through inspection and advice in support of the vision and strategic direction set out by the Welsh Assembly Government. Estyn also plays a key role in the development of the evidence base used by the Welsh Assembly Government in the formulation and evaluation of education and training policy.

Similarly in Scotland, Her Majesty's Inspectorate of Education (HMIE) undertake programmes of inspection of adult learning in colleges and community learning. HMIE are concerned both with the quality of provision and with advising on improvement.

2.3.1 Assessment of the learning outcomes of ALE

Most programmes in publicly funded institutions are described in outcome terms and these definitions are used in assessing their quality. In Higher Education, outcomes are defined by institutions as part of a validation process carried out with external assessors when courses are designed. In Further Education, on the other hand, they are generally defined by external Awarding Bodies, in partnership often with employers. Individual learner performance is then assessed through testing and examination against those specifications. Moves are currently in progress to increase the influence of employers over the specification of qualifications through Sector Skills Councils.

Individual achievement is assessed for all learners, and institutions collect and return data to the appropriate national bodies (either the Higher Education Statistics Agency or the Learning and Skills Council). This data is used not only to assess and accredit the achievement of individual learners, but also to measure the performance of individual institutions; to measure progress towards the Government's targets; in inspection and audit processes; and in funding.

The processes of developing and describing learning outcomes are different in further and higher education:

In Higher Education

In 1997 a National Inquiry into Higher Education chaired by Lord Dearing called for "greater explicitness and clarity about standards and the levels of achievement required for different awards". In response, the Quality Assurance Agency worked with the higher education sector and other stakeholders to create a national qualification framework; a national set of subject benchmark statements; and a framework for institutional programme specifications.

The framework for higher education qualifications aimed to make it easier to understand higher education *qualifications*, by describing the achievements and attributes represented by the main titles such as "bachelors degree with honours", "masters degree" and "doctorate". By setting out the attributes and abilities that can be expected of the holder of a qualification, the frameworks help students and employers understand the meaning and level of qualifications, and provide public assurance that qualifications bearing similar titles represent similar levels of achievement. There is a qualifications framework for England, Wales and Northern Ireland, and a separate one for Scotland, which is part of a wider Scottish Credit and Qualifications Framework. All are linked to the framework set in the Bologna Agreement on Higher Education Qualifications.

Subject benchmark statements set out expectations about standards of degrees in a range of *subject areas*. They describe the conceptual framework that gives a discipline its coherence and identity, and define the level of intellectual demand, techniques and skills which can be expected of an Honours graduate in that subject. The statements also assist institutions in designing and validating programmes.

Programme specifications are produced by each institution, defining what knowledge, understanding, skills and other attributes a student will have developed on successfully completing a *specific programme*. They also provide details of teaching and learning methods, assessment and subsequent career opportunities, and set out how the programme relates to the qualifications framework. This allows prospective students to make comparisons and informed choices about the programmes they wish to study and provides useful guidance for recruiters of graduates.

All this work in higher education is now to be incorporated into the developing National Credit and Qualification Framework.

In formal and non-formal Further Education

Most programmes in Further Education lead to recognised qualifications, issued by national Awarding Bodies (rather than the institutions themselves, as in HE). Awarding Bodies specify the outcomes for each programme, as well as the methods of assessment. Most relate to the National Qualifications Framework, which describes every qualification in detailed outcome terms.

A particular challenge for an outcomes led approach is the treatment of informal adult education programmes which do not lead to national awards, an area in which the UK has traditionally been strong. An outcomes led approach is problematic for two broad reasons. The first concerns measurement, because many of the outcomes are "soft" and difficult to measure in quantitative terms (like self confidence, social engagement and wellbeing), and there are social benefits whose purpose is not properly measured in terms of individual outcomes.

The second problem concerns identifying ultimate objectives against which to measure progress, because many adults do not set out with a specific outcome in mind, and discover new aspirations in the course of study. Furthermore, assessment of adult learners remains controversial, with many learners and teachers resisting what is perceived to be an irrelevant imposition on "learning for its own sake".

In response to these problems, the Learning and Skills Council worked with NIACE to develop 'process benchmarks', based on a five stage process:

- identifying initial individual learning goals/aims;
- assessing learners' knowledge, understanding or skills at the outset;
- agreeing a set of learning outcomes which could include 'soft' outcomes as well as those specific to the skill or subject area;
- undertaking formative assessment and providing learners with feedback to support their learning;
- assessing and recording the extent to which the planned learning outcomes, and any non-planned but relevant ones, had been achieved.

This process became known as RARPA (Recognising and Recording Progress and Achievement).

2.3.2 Tools and mechanisms used to monitor and evaluate programmes to ensure good quality

Inspection reports are published for each institution and every subject, and an annual report on the state of the overall system is published by the Chief Inspector.

In Further Education

Two processes are used in further education: a national system of inspection, undertaken by Ofsted, and a quantitative performance measurement system. Until 2006 there were two separate Inspectorates, the Office of Standards in Education (Ofsted) for schools and further education for people up to 18, and a separate Adult Learning Inspectorate (ALI), which covered all further education for people over 18, including further education, workbased learning provided by private sector training agencies, and non-vocational adult education. In 2007 ALI was merged into Ofsted, which uses a Common Inspection Framework created under the Learning and Skills Act of 2000, and supported by a set of handbooks for different sectors of education.

All FE Colleges have been subject to external inspection by Ofsted and ALI every four years since 1993. This was extended to Workbased learning in 1996, and to non-formal adult education in 2002, but there is now a move away from this model towards 'self regulation'. This involves internal self-assessment by tutors, managers, leaders, and at an organisational level – an annual self-assessment report (SAR) must be submitted by LSC funded providers. This is used to inform inspection by Ofsted, who sample provision and test out the judgements in the SAR to see whether they concur. If they do, the judgements are then formally confirmed as "soundly based."

Prior to an inspection visit, Inspectors receive data reports about the learner success rates gathered through the Individual Learner Record (ILR) which provides a wide range of data on every funded learner. For high performing colleges data of this kind forms a substantial part of the evidence base for their judgements.

The LSC also scrutinises the achievements/success rates of learners. Where these fall below national thresholds/benchmarks the LSC can issue a Notice to Improve which can result in funding being removed if there is no improvement. The thresholds – 'minimum levels of performance' – are raised each year. Prior to recent changes there were national 'floor targets' in relation to learners' success in gaining qualifications.

The LSC is currently developing a performance management framework called *Framework for Excellence*. This will measure institutional performance in three "performance dimensions", each of which has a small number of performance measures. This is a key aspect of how the success of a provider organisation is measured. The Framework is shown below in Table 6.

In Higher Education

In England a process of "Institutional Audit" was introduced in 2003, replacing a more complex, and time consuming, previous process. Its purpose is to ensure that institutions are:

- providing higher education, awards and qualifications of an acceptable quality and an appropriate academic standard; and (where relevant)
- exercising their legal powers to award degrees in a proper manner.

All English higher education institutions were audited between 2003 and 2005; and audits now take place on a six-year cycle.

Institutional audit combines scrutiny of internal quality assurance systems at institutional level, with a more detailed investigation at discipline (subject) level of whether those systems are operating as intended. Before the audit visit, the institution produces self evaluation documents (SEDs), one for the whole institution and one for a sample of academic disciplines. SEDs are key reference points for audit teams during the visit.

Table 6 Performance dimensions of the FE Framework for Excellence

Dimension	Key performance area	Performance indicator	Measures
Responsiveness	Responsiveness to Learners	Learner views Learner destinations	Learner views survey results Employment, or further learning
	Responsiveness to employers	Employer views	Employer views survey results
		Amount of training provided to employers Training Quality standard	Amount of training delivered in an academic year
Effectiveness	Quality of outcomes	Qualification success rates	Success on: –FE short courses, –FE long courses (excluding A levels) –A levels (inc A2 & AS) –Apprenticeship completion rates (including advanced app) –Train to Gain Qualification Success Rates
	Quality of provision	Inspection Grade	
Finance	Financial Health	Solvency	Finance Records for colleges. Latest available statutory financial statements (for other providers in scope)
		Status	
		Sustainability	
	Financial control	Financial Management and Control Evaluation	
	Use of resources	Funding economy	Proportion of income spent on priority provision
		Resource efficiency	Delivery against funding allocated Funding per successful outcome Benchmarked expenditure
		Capital	Provider investment in capital

Assessment of the institution's quality assurance is made on a three point scale (from "broad confidence" to "no confidence" in the in the quality of the institution's provision), and full reports are published, with recommendations and a summary for the general public.

Students are central to the process of institutional audit. For each audit, the representative body (usually the Students' Union) has the opportunity to participate in the key meetings and to provide the audit team with a written submission.

2.3.3 Use of the results for a) legislation, b) policy formulation, and c) programme development

The large volume of performance data gathered through the Higher Education Statistical Agency (HESA) and the LSC is regularly used by policymakers when planning legislation and policies. An example is the emergence of a "lighter touch" approach to quality assurance, in view of the evidence of improving quality in most institutions. Institutions are encouraged to use the data for improvement of programme design and delivery.

2.3.4 Benchmarks in relation to outcomes of ALE

At national level a set of 30 targets exist for Government as a whole (the Public Sector Agreements). Government agrees them through negotiation between the Treasury and each Department during the three yearly Comprehensive Spending Review. Each has a set of agreed Indicators, accompanied by much more detailed measures and targets. In relation to ALE the key indicators are numbers 2, 14 and 15 (see Table 7 and Annex 7).

However, at least nine others have important implications for adult learning, including those relating to economic productivity; regional economic performance; employment opportunities (especially for disadvantaged groups); the social class divide in educational performance; poverty reduction; and social cohesion.

Table 7 Public Service Agreements related to adult learning

PSA	Agreement	Indicator
2	Improve the skills of the population, on the way to ensuring a world-class skills base by 2020	1. Proportion of people working age achieving functional literacy and numeracy skills 2. Proportion of working age adults qualified to at least full Level 2 3. Proportion of working age adults qualified to at least full Level 3 4. Proportion of apprentices who complete the full apprentice framework 5. Proportion of working age adults qualified to Level 4 and above 6. Higher Education participation rate
14	Increase the number of children and young people on the path to success	1. Reduce the percentage of 16–18-year-olds not in education, employment or training (NEET)
15	Address the disadvantage that individuals experience because of their gender, race, disability, age, sexual orientation, religion or belief	1. Participation in public life by women, ethnic minorities, disabled people and young people

In further education, benchmarks for existing provision are set in the *Framework for Excellence*. In higher education, benchmarks for existing provision are set in the Subject Benchmark framework, and institutions benchmark against each other through the outcome of Institutional Audits. There is also a strong tradition of "league tables" of institutions, departments and courses created and publicised by the media, using published quality information. However, this tends to focus heavily on young entrants to higher education, and rarely specifically examines the performance of mature learners.

2.4 Adult educators'/facilitators' status and training

2.4.1 Educational qualifications/training for adult educators/facilitators

Once again, the initial training and continuing professional development of teachers is different in further and higher education.

In Further Education

Most teachers in Further Education are experienced in their field, and many have undertaken roles as supervisors, mentors or workplace trainers before embarking on their formal training as teachers. When they begin formal training for national teaching qualifications, most are already employed as full-time or part-time FE teachers. Their initial teacher training (ITT) courses include a mix of taught and practice elements. The taught element usually involves attending a part-time course, either at the college where they are employed as teachers or at another local college. The practice element takes place in the college where they are employed as teachers or in relevant industrial settings, especially in vocational areas such as in construction and catering.

In 2001, new national regulations were introduced requiring FE teachers to obtain a teaching qualification based on National Standards for teaching and supporting learning. Qualifications based on the National Standards are offered by both higher education institutions (HEI) and national awarding bodies.

In response to a review of teacher training carried out by Inspectors from Her Majesty's Inspectors of Schools (HMI) and the Adult Learning Inspectorate (ALI), in 2003, the Department for Education and Skills (DfES) launched a major national consultation on the reform of ITT in FE and the wider LSC sector, after which it announced, major reforms to the system in the 2006 FE White Paper, *Further Education: Raising Skills, Improving Life Changes*. To be employed as a teacher in FE in England an individual must now have at least a Level 3 qualification (ISCED 3) in the subject (for some academic subjects a University degree is required), as well as a teaching qualification recognised by the Sector Skills Council for FE (Lifelong Learning UK – LLUK).

LLUK is responsible for implementing the 2007 Further Education Workforce Strategy, which aims to support all colleges and learning providers in implementing their own local workforce plans to support the delivery of provision for young people, adults and employers. The new qualifications (and others under development) are a key part of this strategy. The

Teachers Qualification Framework which LLUK has developed includes qualifications for various kinds of teaching and non-teaching staff (in Learning Support, e-Learning, Assessment and in Leadership & Management).

Courses for Further Education teachers are offered by Universities and Colleges on a full and part-time basis, and all trainees are required to have practical teaching experience during their training. In FE, the Institute for Learning is the national professional body for Adult and Community Learning, Emergency and Public Services, Further Education Colleges, Ministry of Defence/Armed Services, the Voluntary Sector and Work-based Learning. It publishes a code of professional practice, and awards "Licensed Practitioner" status to qualified teachers.

The new LLUK teaching qualifications introduced in September 2007 replaced all previous qualifications. They consist of

- The Award in Preparing to Teach in the Lifelong Learning Sector (Level 3): is a short introductory course, designed as an initial 'baseline' or 'passport' qualification that recognises a minimum set of skills and knowledge that teachers will need in order to begin work as a teacher in the sector. This small Award (6 credits at Level 3) will become a requirement for all new staff, and will be particularly important for part-time teachers of adults entering the profession from August 2008.
- The Certificate in Teaching in the Lifelong Learning Sector (Level 4): is targeted at staff who are teaching for some of their time, together with other (e.g. technical or managerial) roles. The 30-credit Certificate will be a useful qualification for adult educators playing a number of roles (including teaching) in, for example, small community-based providers of learning for adults.
- The Diploma in Teaching in the Lifelong Learning Sector (Level 5): is a larger (120 credit)[75] qualification. Leading to Qualified Teacher (Learning and Skills) status. It is offered primarily by HE Institutions (the Award and Certificate are offered mainly by Awarding Bodies). This is the minimum qualification to be employed as a full teacher.

In addition to these initial qualifications, there is a range of other kinds of staff development for serving teachers, and all full time teachers in further education are entitled to 30 hours release from work a year for continuing professional development learning, and this entitlement is available to part-time teachers on a pro-rata basis.

In Scotland, training for FE lecturers is not mandatory, but most lecturers in Scotland's Colleges undertake the Teaching Qualification (Further Education) TQ(FE) whilst in employment, sometimes following achievement of a work-based Initial Teacher Training Professional Development Award (PDA) delivered by an approved college. A pre-service route to the TQ (FE) also exists, approved by the Scottish Government in consultation with the General Teaching Council for Scotland. (see http://www.fepdfscotland.co.uk/). A Continuing Professional Development (CPD) framework also exists for already qualified staff.

---

75 120 credits is the volume equivalent to a year of full-time higher education study.

In Higher Education

There is no national requirement for teaching staff in higher education to hold a teaching qualification, but over the last decade it has become the normal expectation for new staff, encouraged by the Higher Education Academy (HEA), who have been developing in service and initial teacher training for academic staff. The form of training and the requirements to teach are set by individual institutions, who generally train their own staff, through courses approved by HEA. Successful completion of HEA recognised courses leads to "Registered Practitioner" status (effectively a nationally recognised teaching qualification).

There are particular problems about imposing teaching qualifications on the large body of part-time teachers in higher education, and work is in progress in HEA to understand these issues, and develop appropriate responses. The Academy has identified a typology of part-time teachers, with each category having distinct training needs:

- Part-time teachers carrying out a very limited role e.g. one off inputs to programmes
- Inexperienced teachers already present in the HEI (often postgraduate students) deployed to offer defined narrow inputs to teaching.
- Inexperienced teachers as new staff in the HEI deployed to offer defined narrow inputs to teaching (e.g. with particular technical or specialised subject expertise)
- Experienced part-time teachers who have other commitments which place restrictions on their availability and who wish to undertake a limited set of teaching roles
- Inexperienced or experienced part-time teachers who aspire to carrying out all forms of teaching activity (but who also may have competing commitments)
- Fractional teaching staff who have entitlement and access to same opportunities and infrastructure as full-time colleagues

In Work-based Learning

In the Private Training Organisation (PTO) sector, subject qualifications of teaching and teaching related staff range from an apprenticeship to postgraduate qualifications. Teaching qualifications tend to be within a narrow range – the City and Guilds Stage 1 and 2 qualification or the Level 3/4 learning and development (L&D) awards. LLUK is currently overseeing the conversion of the old Training and Development Lead Body (TDLB) units to conform to the new standards for teaching in FE. The LSC, which is a major funder of such providers, has been actively encouraging them to adopt the new awards for their staff, and although they only apply to public sector FE Colleges at present, the intention is that the regulations will, over time come to apply to the wider sector.

2.4.2 Adult education as a specific profession

Adult education is not generally, or legally, identified as a separate field. Adults are taught in Higher, Further, Workbased and Community institutions and settings, and their qualifications, status and terms of employment are based on these settings, not on being teachers of adults. Some Universities have in the past specialised in training of teachers of adults, but the number of such courses has diminished markedly in recent years.

2.4.3 The proportion of adult educators/facilitators in relation to the overall number of teaching personnel in your country.

This number is impossible to define clearly, since many institutions provide for a wide age range, and many teachers will spend some time with adults and some with adolescents, often in mixed age groups. This is also a volatile workforce, with many people taking on part-time teaching roles as part of, or in addition to their main employment, sometimes for a short period only.

The total FE teaching workforce comprised (in England at 2005/6) 125,400 individuals, of whom 50,180 were full time, and 75,220 part-time. This is equivalent to 74,000 full time staff. In addition there were 32,000 "support" staff, who undertake some form of teaching role.

The total HE academic workforce (2005/6) was 164,870 individuals. In addition there were 80,930 "atypical" staff – people who undertake some form of academic role but not under a normal academic contract. By comparison, the total school workforce (at 2005–6) was 429,600 individuals.

Informed observers suggest that Private Training Organisations may also employ around 25,000 staff (including teaching related staff like assessors and advisers), but no national data is collected.

A national inquiry, convened by NIACE, into the position of disabled staff in lifelong learning reported in 2008. It found a systemic failure in both policy and practice to address the needs of disabled staff, and suggested that many providers were not complying with the requirements of the Disability Discrimination Act. Government has promised to take steps to address this issue.

2.4.4 Terms of employment and remuneration in ALE

Teachers of adults are employed on the terms applying to their particular sector (FE, HE, Community Learning, and Workbased Learning). In the first three, which are public sector employers, most staff are paid on nationally agreed pay scales. In the case of workbased learning, conditions are set by the individual (private sector) employer. Most full time, and some part-time staff in FE and HE are employed on permanent contracts. In community learning a much larger proportion are on temporary or casual contracts, and sometimes not paid on national scales.

In Wales, the remuneration of FE staff is now aligned to the national pay scales and awards which apply to schools.

3 Research, innovation and good practice

3.1 Research studies of adult learning

3.1.1 Key studies in adult education within the last five years

During the last decade UK Government's increased interest in evidence based policymaking has led to a growth in spending on research into post school education, to support both policymaking and practice.

In 1999 Government created a National Educational Research Forum, with representation from across all levels of education and training, to advise on the development of a more coherent strategy for educational research. The Forum examined funding, priorities, quality, impact and capacity, and reported to the Secretary of State in 2006. It recommended the creation of a national Evidence Centre for Education, and the development of programmes which combine research and development. A consortium of national agencies involved in further education has subsequently been formed. Government also convenes an annual conference to bring together researchers and civil servants to discuss research findings and emerging policy concerns.

Overall investment in educational research (at all ages) has been increasing, and both Government and the Research Councils[76] have concentrated resources on a small number of major funded programmes in areas of core policy interest. This approach has the advantage of building and maintaining sustainable knowledge bases in key policy areas, but may have reduced the amount of more speculative "blue skies" research in fields which are not currently seen as priorities by either Government or the Research Councils. It has also tended to concentrate funded research in a relatively small number of University Departments.

Broadly, publicly funded research into adult learning can be divided into four types:

■ Academic research
■ Government research
■ Practice based research
■ Underpinning data collection and analysis

76 The Research Councils administer Government funding for research, mainly carried out by Universities. They respond to broad trends in policy interest, but they are independent, and sometimes fund work which is critical of, Government policy.

Academic research

"Academic" research is funded mainly through national research funding bodies, and in some cases directly through Government, usually investigating relatively long term and under–pinning issues:

- the National Research Councils, which allocate public funds to major academic research in all fields, have created specific programmes to examine issues to do with learning. The Economic and Social Research Council fund most of this work. Since 1997, its three largest programmes relevant to adult learning are:
- the **Learning Society Research Programme** (1994–2000) to study the relationship between learning and economic success, and the associated policy implications;
- the **Teaching and Learning Research Programme** (TLRP – 2000–2011) to study the processes of learning and its outcomes;
- the **Centre on Skills, Knowledge and Organisational Performance** (SKOPE – 1998–2013) to study the relationship between economic performance, learning and work in adult life.
- the **Centre for Learning and Life Chances in Knowledge Economies and Societies** (LLAKES – 2008–2013) to study the role of lifelong learning in promoting economic competitiveness and social cohesion, and in mediating the interactions between the two domains.
- A series of research centres, funded directly by Government, and housed in University Departments, have been created to examine specific areas of policy related knowledge. Several of them draw on the important data gathered in the four major longitudinal cohort studies, the first of which has now been collecting data at regular intervals since the cohort was born in 1946. These large datasets have made it possible to map much more clearly the relationship between education and a range of social and economic outcomes. The five Centres with key interests in adult learning are:
- Centre for the Wider Benefits of Learning – examines the non-economic benefits derived from learning at all ages;
- Centre for the Economics of Education – studies the economic impact of education, and its cost effectiveness;
- Centre for Longitudinal Studies – holds and studies data from three of the four major national longitudinal population studies;
- National Research and Development Centre for Adult Literacy and Numeracy – studies the teaching of literacy and numeracy (now absorbed into the Institute of Education, London University);
- Evidence for Policy and Practice Coordinating Centre (the EPPI Centre) – carries out systematic studies of research evidence on key policy areas, and develops research methodology.
- There are three further Centres based in Scotland, but with a wider remit:
- Centre for Research in Lifelong Learning – engages in a range of research and related activities to inform policy and provision in the field of lifelong learning in the post-compulsory sector in Scotland and beyond
- Centre for Research and Development in Adult and Lifelong Learning – engages in research related to the role of adult education and lifelong learning in achieving social

justice, social inclusion and poverty reduction
- PASCAL Observatory – undertakes research in the fields of place management, social capital and lifelong learning.

■ Three surveys, conducted over a decade, have examined attitudes to work, with the results reported in 2007 in Skills at Work 1986–2006. Each survey examined 4800 people, exploring the relationships between skills, qualifications, earnings, training and task discretion at work. It found, over the decade, a striking decline in reported task discretion at work in Britain, which was not matched by a similar pattern in research from comparable countries.

Government research

Government research is carried out by, or commissioned directly by Government, usually to evaluate particular policy interventions;

■ **Directly funded Government research**, commissioned from public and private sector researchers to investigate specific policy issues, and or to evaluate the impact of policies.

■ **The Foresight programme** of the Office of the Government Chief Scientist, is currently carrying out a major multidisciplinary review of the social and economic implications of current research on mental capacity (ranging from neurosciences to sociology).

■ The **funding bodies for Further and for Higher Education** commission research into their own provision. Particular priority has been given to studying the impact of policy on widening access to education and training.

■ The **Sector Skills Development Agency (SSDA)** provided support to the Sector Skills Councils, including carrying out and commissioning research into a range of workforce issues, including the annual Employer Skills Survey, and studies of future labour market skills needs. (the work of the SSDA has now transferred to the UK Commission for Employment and Skills – UKCES)

Practice-based research

"Practice based" research is carried out in close conjunction with practice, and active involvement of practitioners, is usually undertaken by intermediary bodies – NGOs and policy "think tanks". Here research is more closely engaged with the development and evaluation of educational practice and policy.

■ **The National Institute of Adult Continuing Education (NIACE)**: has a large force of staff engaged in project and research work in adult learning, including more than 60 such projects since 1998, on topics ranging from access to accreditation for learning in the voluntary sector, and evaluation of family literacy programmes for offenders, to the role of employee development schemes, and the impact of learning on health. This work is generally funded by Government, the Funding Councils, or by charities with an interest in learning or in social exclusion

■ **The Learning and Skills Development Agency** was funded by Government to provide developmental support to the Further Education sector, developing and evaluating strategies, resources and practice. In 2006 LSDA's functions were divided between two new bodies, the Quality Improvement Agency (QIA)[77] and the Learning and Skills Network (LSN)[78]. The QIA was responsible for quality improvement across the learning and skills sector, while the LSN carried out research, training and consultancy work

- **The Quality Improvement Agency (QIA).** QIA's remit was to help providers respond to government strategic priorities for learning and skills, by commissioning and funding research, programmes and services to support performance improvement and strategic change. This included programmes on Subject Learning Coaches, and Quality in *Skills for Life* work. In June 2008, QIA merged with the Centre for Excellence in Leadership (a leadership support agency in Further Education) to form the new Learning and Skills Improvement Service (LSIS)
- LSN's work included support for programmes on: Key Skills, Vocational Learning, E-Learning and Technology, and Centres of Vocational Excellence
- **The Chartered Institute of Personnel Development**: is the professional body for professionals working in Human Resource Development. It carries out a substantial programme of research into personnel management and development, including education and training.

Underpinning routine data collection and analysis

Underpinning routine data collection produces regular quantitative reports, and provides material for a range of analysis by Government and academic researchers. Such data includes:

- **Routine data collection on further and higher education** has been expanded and improved, and the resulting data has been made more accessible to academic researchers and policymakers. In Further Education, the Individual Student Record gathers detailed demographic data on all students, their qualifications and circumstances, the courses they enrol on and the qualifications they achieve. This makes it possible to examine patterns of participation and career progression by institution, course and personal characteristics. The Higher Education Statistical Agency (HESA) collects and analyses similar data on higher education students, from their initial application for entry to their post graduation careers. Both also run annual student satisfaction surveys to monitor the quality of the student experience of higher education.
- **National social surveys**. In addition to these specific programmes, Government also funds major national surveys which gather data on individuals, including their qualifications and educational experience. These surveys are managed by the Office of National Statistics, under a charter which guarantees its independence of Government. Survey data is made freely available to the general public and to researchers The most relevant are:
- the **Labour Force Survey** – a quarterly survey of 120,000 people over 16;[79]

77 www.qia.org.uk
78 www.lsneducation.org.uk
79 www.statistics.gov.uk/StatBase/Source.asp?vlnk=358&more=Y#general

- the Annual Population Survey, which draws on the LFS sample to produce a quarterly report on 375,000 people;
- the British Household Panel Survey an annual survey of adults in 5,500 households;[80]
- the National Adult Learning Survey (four surveys of 6,500 adults, carried out between 1997 and 2002);
- other national bodies, including the NIACE **Adult Learners Survey** (an annual survey of 5,000 adults, funded by the European Social Fund as part of Adult Learners Week);
- The national **Employer Skills Survey** is conducted annually to examine the views of around 75,000 employers on issues to do with skills and business needs;
- The Future Skills Wales (2005) survey covered 6,719 employers covering all business sectors in Wales in order to provide reliable information on the skill deficiencies which employers in Wales experience;
- Similarly, regular labour market statistics and analysis in Scotland are produced by Futureskills Scotland, part of Scottish Enterprise.

Publications

The findings of this very large body of research are disseminated through a large range of academic journals and practitioner publications, published online and in hard copy by commercial publishers and NIACE. A number of Universities also have Departments which specialise in the study of post-school education and training, and offer postgraduate study at Masters and Doctoral levels.

3.1.2 The major questions addressed and prompted by these studies

The key questions relate to the major themes of public policy: economic productivity and social inclusion. They can be summarised as:

■ What contribution do learning and qualifications make to economic productivity? Includes studies aimed at identifying kinds of learning, kinds of workplace or learner, in particular sectors etc.

■ What is the role of learning in overcoming social exclusion? Includes studies of economic and social disadvantage across the lifecourse; of strategies for widening participation in higher education

■ What strategies attract learners, especially the socially and educationally disadvantaged, to participate in priority programmes (Skills for Life, Level 2 vocational programmes and higher education)

---

80 http://www.statistics.gov.uk/STATBASE/Source.asp?vlnk=1308&More=Y

3.1.3 Key findings

Some of the more important findings in terms of policy impact include:

- That participation in adult education can be shown to contribute to a range of specific social objectives. It leads to improved health (especially reduced depression and obesity) , reduced crime, increased participation in political and community life, and reduction in politically extreme attitudes;
- The critical impact of pre-school learning on life chances. Education alone has a limited impact on the major issues of social exclusion. The influence of social background on educational performance (and hence later life chances) begins to be evident very early. By the time children enter school it is already the dominant influence, and is a major influence on the likelihood of later participation in adult learning;
- The importance of generic skills to employability;
- The importance of informal learning in the workplace. Much, if not most, of the most important work related learning which people undertake takes place outside formal courses, through informal networks, supervision, trial and error. More learning, and more productive learning, happens in "expansive" working cultures;
- The limited impact of information technologies on education. New technologies can make some kinds of knowledge, and some learning opportunities more accessible, but they have not transformed formal or informal learning in the way many people anticipated a decade ago. In general they tend to reinforce existing inequalities in access and achievement, although targeted adult education can enable some people to catch up with the more fortunate peers. Integrating new technologies into whole institutional strategies is much more difficult than using them to enhance learning on particular programmes;
- The tendency of initiatives to widen participation to draw in those immediately below the entry threshold. Most initiatives to widen participation have tended to draw in those on the margins of privileged groups, rather than to transform access to education. For example with regards to widening participation in Higher Education less progress than required has been made;
- That effective techniques and strategies for teaching numeracy and literacy are very different. The traditional view that all basic skills are alike is misleading. The techniques necessary for teaching and learning numeracy are very different from those for literacy;
- The family is a powerful motivator for learning, especially for young parents;
- Formative assessment can be very important in improving the quality of teaching and learning, but is not widely understood by teachers, and many adult learners are resistant to assessment.

Some examples of research findings

The following section comments on a sample of major research issues examined in the last decade:

■ The impact of learning on economic productivity

A wealth of research evidence demonstrates the link between qualifications and earnings and employability in the UK. Generally speaking, those with higher qualifications are much more likely to be in employment, and earn higher wages, than those with lower level qualifications. More qualified individuals are also much more likely to undertake further learning.

While much of this research is usually interpreted as showing the earnings and employment returns to gaining qualifications while young, there is also substantial evidence showing that qualifications gained in adulthood have a positive impact. For example, the Centre for the Economics of Education found that the returns to some vocational Level 2 qualifications are around the same for those who gain them over the age of 25 as for those who gain them at a younger age. The Centre for Economic Performance also found that there are considerable employment benefits to gaining Level 2 qualifications for those who leave school with no qualifications.

In addition, the work of the NRDC has demonstrated that there are significant wage gains for people who acquire basic skills qualifications in adult life before the age of 34, and conversely serious financial disadvantages to failure to do this.

However, the SKOPE Consortium's work on the relationship between learning, work and economic performances has produced a strong critique of a qualification based skills policy. It suggests that the most important learning for productivity comes not from formal courses or qualifications but informal learning in the workplace, and is heavily influenced by the way work is organised and managed.

In relation to skills and economic performance the SKOPE work has demonstrated that:

■ Increasing the supply of skills is necessary, but not sufficient, for improving the UK's economic performance, since it is only one of five significant factors;
■ Employers' demand for skill is not uniform across or within employment sectors, and varies according to the firm's particular product market and production strategies;
■ High skills are not the only route to competitive advantage and the choice of competitive strategy will be influenced by a range of in-company and external factors;
■ Sustained policy intervention to support training is necessary because it is unlikely that the sum of rational and efficient decisions by individual employers adds up to a whole that is socially optimal;

NRDC work has shown the clear effect of low basic skills across generations: individuals with poor skills were much more likely to have grown up in low income homes and to have parents who lacked qualifications. Educational disadvantage carried over into the workplace, with 34 year old men with only Entry 2 level literacy (who were six times more likely to have left school with no qualifications than those with Level 1 literacy) suffering four times the level of unemployment, being half as likely ever to have been promoted and less than half as likely to have received any workplace training. They were also excluded from the digital world with men and women at Entry 2 being roughly three times less likely to use a computer or have internet access at home.[81]

■ *The non-economic benefits of adult learning*

The work of the Centre for Wider Benefits of Learning, using the longitudinal cohort datasets, has established some important effects:

- that level of qualification, and participation in courses in adult life is associated with significant health benefits (reduced obesity, depression and smoking)
- that participation in courses in adult life is associated with improved quality of life, reduced political cynicism, increased racial tolerance, increased social engagement and willingness to vote

■ *Strategies for engaging adults with basic skills needs in learning*

NRDC work has found that family learning and workplace learning have been particularly effective in reaching adults with low basic skills, although some workplaces leave no time or space for learning, especially for the low skilled. Their work also stresses the importance of:

- learning strategies which take account of the complex nature of adults' lives, particularly where these cause them to dip in and out of formal provision;
- formative assessment;
- attitudinal factors;
- recognising that different strategies may be needed for literacy, numeracy and ESOL.

■ *What prevents people from disadvantaged backgrounds from participating in adult learning?*

The Learning Society programme examined the social determinants of participation in adult learning, and concluded that five factors were very significant, and that in all five, the principal features were determined relatively early in the lifecourse. The five were:

- Time: when born, changing opportunities, salience of qualifications;
- Place: where born and brought up, local opportunities and social expectations, geographical mobility;
- Gender: men report more learning than women, and social expectations of women's learning remain lower;
- Family: social class, educational experience and religion, financial and cultural capital;
- Initial schooling: learner identities;

Research on educational performance has consistently shown that the impact of social class on performance is measurable before the age of 5.

81 NRDC (2007) *Five Years On*

In response to a view that the UK's future economic competitiveness depends on remaining at the leading edge of a high skill economy, Government set a target that 50 per cent of all people should have had some experience of higher education (HE) by the age of 30, and funded a variety of initiatives designed to widen participation. The aim was to significantly widen the socio-economic base of the student body.

The relative failure of policies to widen participation appears to be due largely to inequalities earlier in the education system, rather than financial reform and other factors in HE. In other words, poorer students are much less likely to acquire the necessary qualifications to get into HE in the first place. The effect of policy interventions to widen participation in HE appears to have been to increase take up by people from relatively advantaged backgrounds, rather than to widen the socio-economic base. When tuition fees were introduced for HE there was widespread concern that this might discourage lower income students from applying, but there is little evidence that this has happened.

■ *The role of new technologies in adult learning*

There has been much discussion of the implications of new technologies for adult learning, and adult access to computers and the Internet has expanded very rapidly, especially among older people, who are keen to keep up with their children and grandchildren. Indeed, ICT learning accounts for over 40 per cent of all learning by people over 65. However, most of the learning which has taken place has been about the technology itself, rather than using the technology as a vehicle for learning. The highest demand at Learndirect centres, which provide local free access to short online courses has been for courses on how to use ICTs (rather than courses using ICTs).

More worryingly, the evidence is strong that, despite many efforts to use technology to overcome social exclusion, it has tended to reinforce social divisions, with the people who use the internet for learning, or for gathering and using information, tending to be those with the highest levels of previous education, and the best access to traditional learning programmes.

The Cardiff University study of this issue in 2004, Adult Learning@Home, found that:[82]

■ The key determinant of learning in later life is experience of work and family life as an adult, rather than access to ICTs.

■ Although only eight per cent of those surveyed could be classed as "excluded" from computers and the Internet, 48 per cent had not used a computer during the past 12 months.

■ Only 11 per cent of respondents reported using a computer in a public location such as a library, compared to 44 per cent using one at home and 32 per cent in the workplace.

■ Using the Internet to learn a language or other new skill was secondary to communicating with family and friends, producing documents and searching for specific information and general knowledge.

- The key factor underlying the success of ICT-based learning is an individual's motivation and self-discipline.
- E-learning was most often concerned with the technology itself, rather than a means to learn something else. The researchers concluded that ICTs appear to reinforce existing patterns of learning and were mainly of benefit to people who were already learners, or who would have become learners without the availability of ICT.
- Adult learning through ICTs was largely informal and unstructured, even when it took place at work or in educational institutions. It was often augmented by books, television programmes and help and advice from others.
- Most adults seem to create a use for the technology rather than the technology solving some existing problem or lack in their lives. This was most obvious in hobby and leisure use, such as adults producing greetings cards.

■ What does recent research tell us about effective "pedagogy"?

The Teaching and Learning Research Programme has developed a set of ten "evidence-informed pedagogic principles" derived from its 100 research projects and related activities to study learners of all ages. The TLRP team believe that these principles apply across all age ranges and contexts. They are shown in Annex 6.

3.1.3 Influence of findings on policies and practice

Perhaps the most influential piece of work of the decade was carried out by the Performance and Innovation Unit of the Cabinet Office in preparation for the National Skills Strategy paper *In Demand: Adult Skills in the 21st Century* published in 2002. This found clear evidence of the importance of basic skills and qualifications up to Level 2 (ISCED 2) to individual life chances, earnings and productivity. However, it also found that neither employers nor employees were likely to invest in training at this level, whereas they would both invest in training for higher-level learning.

This provided the rationale for the main thrust of skills policy since 2000, which is to target public funding on qualifications at this level, where market failure is deemed to be most severe, with an impact on both economic performance and social inclusion. One consequence of this policy has been to divert funding from other areas of education and training.

There have been a number of critiques of this evidence, and academic debate continues. For example there is evidence that a large part of the benefit of Level 2 qualifications derives from the literacy and numeracy elements of Level 2 qualifications.

Also, some of the latest evidence shows a strong positive average earnings returns for NVQ2 qualifications. This contrasts with previous evidence based on cross-sectional data that has found average earnings returns to NVQ2 to be negligible. This may be because the longitudinal nature of the data allows the researchers to better control for the unobservable characteristics of individuals gaining qualifications. In this instance, formal qualifications are used as a proxy for the skills which employers require or use, or for the skills which employees themselves report using, many of which are derived from unaccredited informal workplace learning.

There is also a need to recognise the significance of skills obsolescence, which is caused by a number of factors including atrophy (failure to use); technological and organisational change causing jobs to change. Updating of skills over a lifetime becomes more important. Sector Skills Councils have a role in making sure qualifications keep up to date with employer needs. This is particularly relevant in view of the growing policy concern to extend working life and improve the economic contribution of people over 50.

3.2 Innovations and examples of good practice

3.2.1 Policy formulation, financing, teaching/learning methods

Structures of target setting and performance monitoring, at national and institutional level

■ *Qualifications reform*

In 2008 a new Qualifications and Credit Framework (QCF) will begin operation, after two years of trialling. The Framework aims to make the current adult vocational qualifications system easier to understand, and make it easier for learners to progress. It will also be used in performance monitoring and funding mechanisms.

The framework will initially include only post-19 vocational qualifications, although it has been developed to be able to extend to cover general (academic) qualifications and qualifications for 14–19 year olds. The Framework attaches credit to units of qualifications at one of nine levels. Every qualification will be described in terms of:

- level – Entry or Level 1 to level 8 (Doctoral);
- size/volume of work – Awards (initially set at 1–12 credits, or 10–120 guided learning hours), Certificates (13–36) and Diplomas (37+);
- content.

A development programme is being planned, with a view to including all vocational qualifications in the framework by 2010, and likely extension to general (academic) and 14–19 qualifications by 2014. Alongside this will be a programme of support, including

- implementation of an ICT system to support the QCF;
- development of new and revision of needed existing vocational qualifications in accordance with the new QCF regulatory arrangements;
- in England, trialling of new LSC funding arrangements to support the QCF;
- in England, a programme of support to assist providers to deliver QCF qualifications;
- piloting of a new 'Credit Success Rate' measure for providers
- detailed planning to prepare for the submission of general qualifications

The QCF has been developed to align with the existing Scottish Credit & Qualifications Framework.

■ *Foundation Degrees*

In the 1990s Government, concerned to promote a high skills economy, declared its intention to raise participation in higher education to 50 per cent of the 18–30 age group However, they also wished to increase the vocational relevance of higher education programmes, and increase employer engagement in course design to achieve this.

To address these objectives a new qualification, the Foundation Degree,[83] was introduced. These are two year full time (or equivalent part-time) higher education qualifications, designed by Further or Higher Education institutions, usually incorporating a substantial element of practical work experience. In 2007 there were 2500 Foundation Degree programmes, with a further 800 in development.

Some Foundation Degrees are provided to current employees of a sponsoring employer, while others are aimed at people seeking a higher education qualification in a specific vocational field. For many graduates a Foundation Degree leads directly to employment in the relevant industry of firm, but Foundation Degrees are also designed to provide a vocational route to advanced entry to a full Bachelor's degree, and about half do this.

Since their launch in 2001 the number of Foundation Degree students has risen to 72,000, with a Government target to reach 100,000 by 2010. Two thirds of students are over 21 at entry, and a little over half are women.

■ *Apprenticeships*

During the 1980s a policy decision was taken to run down the traditional apprenticeship model of vocational training for young people, which was seen as time consuming and poorly adapted to current labour market needs. In 1994, Government announced the creation of a new model, the "Modern Apprenticeship" which would operate as an initial vocational qualification, with a strong element of core skills, work experience and employer engagement. From 1997 increased emphasis was placed on the programme and in 2007–8 the number of new apprenticeships was 83,000, including a rising proportion of adults (29,600).

The Leitch Report proposed a target of 400,000 apprenticeships by 2020 (with 190,000 successful completions a year). Government has accepted this, and committed to funding it. The target includes a substantial proportion of adult apprentices, for whom there is high employer demand. Government is increasing central support and incentives for the programme. These include:

■ Clarification of the qualifications of apprentices in line with the national qualification framework;
■ Creating a national apprenticeship support service;
■ More flexibility to adapt to employer needs;
■ Public sector targets and duties to offer apprenticeships;
■ Promotion of apprenticeships in major public strategic projects;
■ Improved information;
■ Clear progression routes from apprenticeship to higher education;

83 http://www.fdf.ac.uk

■ A series of equality measures to ensure equal treatment and address inequality in access.

■ *NHSU*

One of the most radical initiatives of the last decade was NHSU (the "National Health Service University"). This was conceived as a "corporate university" for the Service, which is one of the world's largest employers (with over 1.5 million employees). It was announced in the Labour Party's election manifesto of 2001, and created by the Department of Health in 2003.

It planned to deliver learning programmes, especially aimed at three targets:

■ to raise the skills of the lowest skilled, manual workers, (who are often overlooked in NHS Human Resource policies);

■ to improve the quality of leadership and management across the service

■ to assist the process of strategic change (for example the retraining of nurses to take on some functions previously carried out by doctors, and the implementation of new IT systems across the NHS).

It was hoped that NHSU would lead to greater uniformity of practice, and the dissemination of good practice across a fragmented service nationwide. The expectation was that much of its teaching would be done using state of the art technologies, including online and interactive materials and programmes.

The initiative recruited a large staff of highly motivated people from within the NHS and the broader education and training communities, but encountered some serious difficulties. Existing higher education institutions saw it as a potential threat both to their existing relationships with the NHS, and to the notion of a University itself (which led to it being renamed "NHSU" rather than "NHS University"). NHS professional bodies saw it as a threat to their professional autonomy, and their control over professional standards. The NHS Trusts (the managerial units of the service at local level) saw it as an unnecessary additional complexity in a time of major structural change in the service. It was also inevitable that such ambitious objectives would take time to achieve: materials had to be of high quality, and soundly tested to ensure that they could meet the most severe scrutiny, not only for pedagogy, but for safety, ethics, and medical accuracy. After two years of preparation, the first courses were launched in 2005 (and in the first year the target of 100,000 learners was achieved.

However, despite Ministers' enthusiasm, the Department of Health found it difficult to manage, and resisted the degree of independence implied by the title of "University". In July 2004, when Government undertook a review of a wide range of organisations associated with the NHS, it decided to close NHSU. However, most of the programmes were transferred to other locations in the NHS, and the final evaluation report suggested that perhaps half of the total cost of NHSU (£60m) would be recovered by this process.

■ *National initiatives in technology and learning*

The pace of technological change has continued to accelerate over the last ten years. Its impact on adult education has been driven by a series of government programmes that have targeted parts of the post-16 sector. The initial programmes (National Learning Network) were focused on FE Colleges and addressed three themes:

■ developing infrastructure;
■ providing learning materials;
■ Staff Development.

The NLN programme was advised by and, to a degree, managed by, a partnership of educational providers, government agencies and other interested groups. The partnership produced a national plan for FE Colleges whereby every college was required to develop a strategy for the use of technology. The plan was managed formally by the Learning and Skills Council (LSC). The programme extended the JANET broadband network into all colleges, created a large volume of e-learning content and launched a staff development programme that produced a national network of learning champions.

The NLN programme was later extended into those parts of adult and community learning that were funded through the LSC, followed by Work-Based Learning providers and most recently into Offender Learning. The extension into adult and community learning was preceded by the development of an e-learning strategy for the sector, undertaken by a representative group convened by NIACE. Key lessons learnt from this work included:

■ **E-guides** – the staff development model adopted in ACL involved the training of e-guides who were responsible for supporting, mentoring and developing their peers. By 2008, 2000 e-guides have been trained and they have in turn supported approximately 14,000 other staff. They now form a network of expertise through which good practice and new ideas can flow.
■ **Simple technology** is often very powerful – one of the key technologies in non-formal adult education has been the digital camera, which has been employed to provide feedback, capture outcomes and as a focus for project work.
■ **Developing local strategic plans** helps to engage senior managers at an appropriate level and assist with developing their skills.

Perhaps the most important aspect of the success of introducing e-learning into Adult and Community Learning was the development of a national strategy and implementation plan by representatives from the sector.

In Higher Education, a considerable effort is being undertaken in employing new technology to enhance learning. This has resulted in the development of online programmes, with learners in some cases being recruited from across the world. The developments in Higher Education have been initiated and encouraged through both local and central programmes. The Joint Information and Systems Committee (JISC) is the central organisation through which funds have been managed. The JISC supports in partnership with the LSC, a national network of centres that assist universities, FE Colleges, Adult and Community Learning and other providers with technology related development.

The government agency responsible for support to technology in education, BECTa, is currently producing a new version of its e-learning national policy, *Harnessing Technology*. This policy covers the whole of the education sector and one of its foci is the e-maturity of educational providers, essentially, do they have the skills and understanding to make the most effective use of technology for learning in their whole organisation? The current view is that although considerable effort has been made, only a minority of providers are e-mature. This indicates that although it is relatively straightforward to introduce a degree of e-learning into a single class or programme, to integrate technology across an entire organisation is far more difficult.

Although e-learning is a feature of all types of education at present, its use is partial and there are considerable differences across the whole education sector. Nevertheless, the momentum for change has been established and it will continue to grow and expand.

■ Sectoral learning

Government has, for many years, been concerned to increase employer involvement in education, to try to improve the match between the skills and knowledge which are needed for employment. Recognising the very different requirements of individual employment sectors it announced, in 2003, the intention to create a set of national Sector Skills Councils, each to be run by employers from the relevant sector and with a remit to produce plans for future skills needs, and for training to meet them. 25 Councils were established, and each undertook research to map the skills of the current workforce, to predict future demand for skills and labour, and make proposals for training to meet the needs.

The Councils were supported by a Sector Skills Development Agency (SSDA) which oversaw the production of, and approved, the Sector Skills Agreements which were to drive development in training and qualifications for their sector. SSDA also carried out overarching research into labour market trends and requirements, including the major annual National Employer Skills Survey (which surveys over 74,000 employers). The Agency's *Working Futures*[84] publications series provided an overview of skills needs by sector at national and regional level, as well as of projected demand for qualifications, and SSDA also created a publicly accessible online research database containing the data from all their survey work.[85] This has proved a valuable tool for employer bodies, education providers and academic researchers.

In 2007, in response to the Leitch report on Skills, Government announced that the SSDA would be absorbed into a new employer led body, the UK Commission for Employment and Skills (UKCES), with a remit to support the raising of the UK's skills base, improving productivity and competitiveness, increasing employment and making a contribution to a fairer society. It will play a critical part in securing for the UK the ambitions of achieving a world-class profile on skills by 2020 and the aspiration of an 80 per cent employment rate.

■ Cross-Government coordination of ageing policy

Demographic trends are producing a rapid ageing of the UK population (although less rapid than in some OECD countries). In 2007, the proportion of the population over 65 (16 per cent) exceeded the proportion who were under 16, and the proportion over 65 is expected to

84 Dickerson, Homenidou and Wilson (2006) *Working Futures 2004–2014: National Report* http://www.ssda. org.uk/PDF/Working%20Future%2020042014%20National%20Summary%20R%2020060215.pdf
85 Sector Skills Matrix http://www.ssdamatrix.org.uk/

rise to 22 per cent by 2031. Furthermore, the proportion over 85 is rising by more than 5 per cent per year. In 2005 Government published a paper "Opportunity Age" which sought to present a coordinated approach to the social and economic implications of these trends, which cut across all Government Departments. It also created a national Partnership Group, which brings together all the relevant Government Departments, with relevant national agencies. This Group has created an Education and Training Committee, which is examining the implications for lifelong learning policy, including the implications of age discrimination law for older learners, the effects of broader educational policy and the collection of data on older learners, both for those in (or aspiring to be in) the workforce, and those who have permanently retired.

In Scotland, a long-term strategy *All our futures – Planning for Scotland with an Ageing Population* was published in March 2007, and among other priorities, identified the need to provide learning opportunities throughout life, both vocational and personal as part of an overall strategy to promote active ageing, and continuing participation in social and economic life for as long as people wish to do so. The strategy proposed the establishment of a National Forum on Ageing to take forward and monitor the implementation of the strategy.

3.2.2 Involvement of learners in programme design, and emergence of learners as partners

Information, advice and guidance

In an increasingly complex and mobile economy and society, it is likely that individuals will need to return to learning a number of times during lifetime to prepare for or manage change in work, personal circumstances and life phases. If an individual is to make effective use of the opportunities available, it is important that he or she has access to reliable information about them, and advice about how to find the most appropriate opportunity for his or her individual circumstances, needs and aspirations.

Since the early 1980s Government and a range of professionals have sought ways of developing a coherent system to provide such advice, generally known as "Information, Advice and Guidance" (IAG). The national *Learndirect* service has built a national database of learning opportunities, in public, voluntary and private sectors, and runs a telephone helpline, and online service to provide individuals with information and advice. The database now holds information on 900,000 courses, and the helpline handles 4,500–6,000 calls every weekday and about 3,000 calls per day at weekends. Advice is offered in 9 languages, and facilities are available for handling enquiries from people with learning difficulties or disabilities. *Learndirect* also provides an enhanced service to people who lack a first Level 3 qualification, are seeking to return to work, in low paid or low skilled work, or are facing redundancy.[86]

Learndirect also established a network of 800 local learning centres, in a wide variety of locations (including high street shops) offering access to and support for some training courses in a wide range of subjects, 75 per cent of them delivered online, with a particular

86 www.learndirect.co.uk

focus on IT and business skills. Since opening in 2000, it has provided some 4.5 million courses to 2 million learners.

Alongside this service Government has created the *Nextsteps* service, which provides face-to-face guidance on careers and learning to adults. The service is funded through the Learning and Skills Council, and delivered through a series of contracts with guidance providers, usually private sector companies created for the purpose.

Although *Learndirect* and *Nextsteps* are the largest services, and provide the bulk of the publicly funded guidance, there is a large and diverse market of agencies working in this field in public, private and voluntary sectors. Some operate only in a particular locality or region, and others nationwide, while some deal with specialised needs. There is a strong private sector of recruitment agencies, some of whom provide advice about qualifications and training to people seeking employment. Some professional bodies provide career guidance to their members or to people seeking to enter the profession. Finally, the Government's own employment service "Jobcentre Plus", which provides employment advice primarily to the unemployed, also provides advice on education and training to its clients.

The staff of these services come from a variety of backgrounds, and are supported by a number of professional bodies. A National Guidance Council was created by the various interested agencies in the 1990s, and this created a quality assurance framework for the services themselves, including a set of service standards (the Matrix Standards) which services can use to demonstrate their quality. Although there is no legal requirement for such services to be recognised, these standards are usually required of agencies seeking support from public funds.

In 2006–7 the Government carried out a Review of Adult Advice and Guidance services with a view to creating a more coherent service. The outcome of this was the decision to create a new national Adult Advancement and Careers Service, to bring together and build on the work of *Nextsteps* and *Learndirect*. This service is being developed progressively over the period 2008–2011, by which time it is expected to be nationally available, with additional funding of £50million pa. A particular feature of this service is to be a focus on supporting people in low skilled jobs to upgrade their skills and jobs.

One challenge which Government faces in creating this service is to ensure that constraints on funding do not lead it to focus attention too heavily on socially excluded groups, leading to it being stigmatised in the public mind, and thus ceasing to be seen as a universal resource. This happened to a parallel initiative, the Connexions service, which sought to provide integrated career, education and social advice to young people, and the Government's Jobcentre Plus service, which exists to assist the unemployed back into work. Both suffer from being stigmatised in public attitudes as services only for the seriously excluded.

87 The paper uses the term "Informal" to embrace both "informal" and "non-formal" learning under the UNESCO definition.

Learning Champions

Another scheme that mobilises learners is the Learning Champions (also known as learning ambassadors, representatives or advocates). These are volunteers or paid employees who promote the benefits of learning locally in their communities to family, friends, colleagues etc and signpost them to suitable courses. Learning champions act as role models and are very effective in reaching out to people who are otherwise disengaged with learning.

Many of the learning champions projects were initiated with funds from the Adult and Community Learning Fund. The Fund launched by Government in 1998 (but closed in 2004) resourced large and small projects in community-based organisations aimed at reaching out to adults who do not normally participate in education.

Learner accounts

For some years there has been interest in ways of making ALE provision more responsive to "customer demand", and this is now an established plank of Government policy. One tool for this is the creation of a system of learner accounts, funded, or part funded, by the State, which would put purchasing power for ALE (or some forms of it) in the hands of individuals.

This approach was first tried in 2000 with a scheme of Individual Learning Accounts, in which individuals could claim up to £150 if they invested £25 or their own money in a virtual "account". They could then use the total sum to buy vocational courses of specified types. The scheme was very successful in stimulating participation, and 2.5 million people took up accounts over the 14-month period that the scheme operated. Unfortunately its success created unsustainable pressure on available funds, and capacity to administer and audit the scheme. As a result the scheme was closed in England and in Scotland (but not in n the National Health Service, and in Wales, where schemes continued). A modified scheme has now been re-introduced in Scotland targeted on those with lower incomes, and also offering some support to those on lower incomes on part-time HE courses. Elsewhere a new scheme is now being piloted on a more modest basis in two regions in the 2007–8 academic year, and funds will only be available to buy programmes above Level 2.

One clear weakness of such a model is that "customers" may be ill informed about the opportunities available, and may make "unwise" purchasing decisions. One way of limiting this risk is the development of good information and advice systems.

Informal learning – the consultation

By international standards, the UK has traditionally had very high levels of participation in informal and non-formal adult learning. However, an unintended consequence of Government policy to focus public funds on vocationally focused qualifications and basic skills has been a substantial decline in participation in informal and non-formal adult education. Government's intention that provision should continue, but with learners contributing a growing proportion of the costs of such programmes as public funding was progressively reduced, has not been realised, and 1.4 million fewer people were participating in 2007–8, compared with three years earlier.

As a consequence, in January 2008, the Department for Innovation, Universities, Skills and Science launched a public consultation on the future of "Informal learning".[87] This starts from the principle that a diversity of such programmes is desirable, but that it cannot be the sole responsibility of the state to pay for it. The paper proposes that the public funds available for such work (currently £210M pa) might be reallocated, possibly to provide a stronger infrastructure to underpin a more diverse market of providers in public, private and third sectors, with more of the cost of programmes being borne by learners themselves.

The consultation, which includes expert seminars with Ministers, closed in June 2008, and was to be followed by a policy paper later in the year.

U3A

During the 1980s a movement to create "Universities of the Third Age" developed across a number of countries. In the UK the model adopted was generally of a collection of self supporting voluntary organisations, each with its own mission and ways of working, but most of them sharing the principle that they existed to serve older people (commonly over 50) and operated through courses taught by their own unpaid members. Thus members would share their expertise and knowledge, minimising the costs to participants.

In the last decade, the organisation has become more structured, through its national body, the Third Age Trust. This provides (with limited funding from Government and a range of other agencies, including charities), support for local groups, each of which retains its individual identity and autonomy, but has access to a library of teaching resources, and guidance on how to organise and operate a group.

In the last few years U3A has seen a rapid expansion in the number of local groups, and in total membership (currently growing at over 12 per cent a year, and currently with 628 local groups and 170,000 learners). This growth coincides with the steep decline in enrolment by older learners in publicly funded programmes.

Unionlearn

In 1998 the *Learning Age* Green Paper set up a Union Learning Fund to promote trade unions' support in the creation of a learning society. In the decade since the work started more than fifteen thousand ordinary trade unionists have been recruited and trained to become union learning representatives (ULRs), encouraging colleagues back into learning. ULRs have statutory rights to time-off for training and carrying out their duties and research has shown that their presence in a workplace leads to significantly higher levels of training.[88]

In May 2006 the Government announced the expansion and development of this model by launching the academy for trade union learning, *UnionLearn*.

The main aims of the academy are:

- to support unions to be become learning organisations;
- to help unions broker learning opportunities for their members;
- and to research union priorities on learning and skills to help influence policy.

88 Leeds University Centre for Employment Relations, Innovation and Change

Unionlearn has played a key role in refining the role and nature of trades unionism, and a key priority is to build a network of 22,000 union learning representatives by 2010 and to have 250,000 learners going through union routes.

National Learner Panel

In November 2006 the English Government set up the National Learner Panel to advise on how proposed changes to Further Education affect learners. The Panel is made up of 18 volunteer learners, whose age ranges from 17 to 67, drawn from across the sector, participating in all types of further education provision. The panel meets four times a year to discuss their views on major issues affecting learners. Since it was set up it has provided Government with a learner's perspective on how to ensure learners' views are taken into account during college inspections, how best to implement reforms aimed at raising the level of skills in the UK and a range of views on proposals to raise the minimum age at which young people can leave education or training. Furthermore in 2007 the Panel together with the LSC and the Framework for Excellence developed a Learner Involvement Strategy with standards and criteria for capturing and responding to learner views across the FE sector. A related mechanism that captures learner views is the National Learner Satisfaction Survey (NLSS), the largest survey of the post-16 learners in England.

3.2.3 Why are the listed examples considered as innovations in the UK?

The examples are all new approaches (in the UK) to six key policy issues.

Bridging the academic-vocational divide

This is a long standing cultural problem for UK (and especially England). Qualifications reform, Foundation Degrees and Apprenticeships are all attempts to make it easier for individuals to combine learning from the two domains, and to progress between them.

Developing a "market" in ALE

This is a major theme underlying Government policy (across many fields) based on the notion that the quality and value for money of services will be better and those services more relevant if individuals and employers have more influence over what is provided and opportunities to choose between providers and opportunities. The involvement of employers in qualification reform, in Foundation Degrees and in Sector Skills Councils all aim to do this for employers, while Learner Accounts give individuals purchasing power in an education market, and developments in advice and guidance provide information and support in making informed choices.

Applying technology to learning

The various initiatives listed all seek to ensure that individuals have better access to ICTs, for learning and life more widely, and that education providers are making best use of them. NHSU was the largest and most ambitious attempt to build an educational institution with technology at core of its processes – the decision to close NHSU was not baaed on failure to achieve this objective.

Coordinating policy across Government departments

Coordination across Departments is a theme of much Government policy in the last ten years, and substantial moves have been made to do this. Coordination of policy on older people is an example of this

Developing new models for informal learning

Traditionally the UK has had a very well developed model of non-formal learning (courses which do not lead to qualifications). It also has a very strong third sector of voluntary and community organisations which provide learning opportunities for their voluntary and paid staff and for their clients. Social change, and the need to support learning directed explicitly to Government economic and social priorities has led to a fundamental review of how the state intervenes to support such activity. The development of a self-help learning model in U3A an example of an innovative approach to this issue.

Improving responsiveness to learner need

The creation of formal mechanisms for consulting learners about policy development through the Adult Learner Panel, ad the encouragement for parallel processes at local level is a new move to increase the responsiveness of the service to learner needs and views

4 Adult literacy

4.1 Literacy definitions and developments

There is no universally agreed definition of "literacy" in the UK. The relevant Government policy for basic skills is laid out in its 2001 Skills for Life strategy.

Skills for Life include reading and writing, but set within a much broader notion of functional competence, and it is on this definition that targets and evaluation are based. Skills for Life were first defined in 2002 as: the ability to read, write and speak in English and to use mathematics at a level necessary to function at work and in society in general.

In 2003 it was agreed to extend the definition to embrace a fourth element, so that the current definition consists of:

- Reading and writing
- Speaking and listening
- Numeracy
- Information and Communication Technology

The Scottish approach to adult literacies adopts a distinctive "social practice" model, which sees literacies as a key dimension of community regeneration and a part of the wider lifelong learning agenda. In Scotland literacy is defined as:

"The ability to read and write and use numeracy, to handle information, to express ideas and opinions, to make decisions and solve problems, as family members, workers, citizens and lifelong learners."

The Scottish approach recognises that:

- literacy and numeracy are complex capabilities rather than a simple set of basic skills
- learners are more likely to develop and retain knowledge, skills and understanding if they see them as relevant to their own context and everyday literacy practices.

In Wales, the Welsh Assembly Government defines basic skills as the ability to read, write and speak in English or Welsh, and to use mathematics at a level necessary to function and progress both in work and in society.

Within the national qualifications framework there are three "entry levels" of qualification below level 1 which are used in Skills for Life. As an example, the following definitions are used for reading literacy:

Table 8 Literacy levels in the National Qualifications Framework

Entry Level 1	Understands short texts with repeated language patterns on familiar topics Can obtain information from common signs and symbols
Entry Level 2	Understands short straightforward texts on familiar topics accurately and independently Can obtain information from short documents, familiar sources and signs and symbols
Entry Level 3	Understands short straightforward texts on familiar topics accurately and independently Can obtain information from everyday sources
Level 1	Understands short straightforward texts on varying length on a variety of topics accurately and independently Can obtain information from different sources
Level 2	Understand a range of texts of varying complexity accurately and independently Can obtain information of varying length and detail from different sources

However, within the UK the term "literacy", and its associated terms "basic education", "basic skills", "key skills" and "core skills" continue to be widely used in a variety of senses. At times they are used to refer to:

■ Reading and writing only – the narrowest definition;
■ Functional competences – a range of competences, including some or all of: reading, writing, speaking, numeracy and information technology skills;
■ Multiple literacies – required to function as a full citizen, which may include 'financial literacy', 'political literacy', 'media literacy', 'health literacy', 'computer literacy', 'legal literacy', 'social literacy', and 'economic literacy';
■ Language skills – to include English language for people whose first language is not English ("English for Speakers of Other Languages", and "English as a Foreign Language")

In an attempt to clarify terminology, NIACE and NRDC, have sought to establish the term "Literacy, language and numeracy" (LLN), to stress the distinction between them in terms of curricula, pedagogies, skills, teaching expertise, and sometimes learners.

4.2 New policies adopted and implemented

Basic skills is the area of adult learning which has seen the largest Government intervention in the last decade, with the launch in 2002 of the Government's *Skills for Life* strategy, and an investment of over £3.5 billion since 2000.

The case for major intervention was made in England in the report *A Fresh Start: Improving Literacy and Numeracy* commissioned by Government, and published in 1999 (known as "The Moser Report" after its chairman). The report drew on the OECD International Adult Literacy Survey of 1997, and argued that some 7 million people (1 in 5 adults) needed to improve their basic skills in one or more areas. The result of this skills deficit, it argued, was social exclusion and economic disadvantage for individuals, and a serious constraint on the economy.

This view was strengthened by subsequent research, including a major survey of 8,700 adults (including formal testing) carried out in 2002/3. This found that 16 per cent of people aged 16–65 (5.2 million) had literacy levels below Level 1 in the qualification framework, and 32 pre cent of unemployed people were handicapped in finding work by low levels of literacy and numeracy.[89]

The Strategy set ambitious targets:

- 750,000 adults to improve their language, literacy and numeracy by 2004 (target exceeded);
- 1.5 million to have improved these skills by 2007;
- 2.5 million to have moved up one level of the national standards framework by 2010.

The Strategy identified a number of specific target groups:

- unemployed people;
- prisoners and ex-offenders;
- people in work, including public sector employees;
- unqualified young people;
- parents supported by the "Sure Start" programme, (a national programme designed to help parents in disadvantaged communities to support their children's' early development);
- people with English language needs (ESOL – English for Speakers of Other Languages).

The Strategy was supported by an Adult Basic Skills Strategy Unit, based in the Department for Education and Skills, and a national Basic Skills Agency,[90] in addition to funding programmes for learners, it included a number of infrastructure investments. These included:

National standards

Separate standards were written for literacy and numeracy, providing a map of the range of skills and capabilities that adults were expected to need in order to function and progress at

89 A parallel Scottish study which found 800,000 people of working age with skills at or below this level.
90 The Basic Skills Agency was merged into NIACE in 2007.

work and in society. Separate curricula were then developed and published for literacy and for numeracy, and later for English language. This was followed by new national qualifications for adults in all three fields.

Promotion and awareness raising

Large scale promotional activity took place, including poster campaigns and national television advertising, highlighting the challenges faced by people with basic skills difficulties A national telephone helpline was established to help people with skills needs to find appropriate programmes. The promotional activities aimed not only to encourage people with needs to come forward for tuition, but to raise awareness more generally, including among staff in key positions in organisations which could assist and refer people to learning, and employers of all kinds, including Government departments. A recent promotional campaign organised by the LSC is seeking to increase the focus on numeracy.

Capacity building

Initial training programmes were developed for teachers working on *Skills for Life* programmes, including qualifications for the large numbers of volunteer and part-time teachers. Standards for such teachers were set in 2000, and have recently been revised. A large programme of continuing professional development, including short courses, workshops and longer programmes leading to accredited qualifications were provided to serving teachers, to maintain and update their skills and knowledge. *Skills for Life* teachers benefit from the national entitlement to 30 hours p.a. continuing professional development.

This work was backed up by the creation of the National Research and Development Centre for Adult Literacy and Numeracy, with a remit to undertake and disseminate research into the development of these skills. The Centre has sponsored a wide range of research studies, and each year it has organised national and international conferences to discuss and disseminate findings to practitioners, policymakers and researchers.

Curriculum

Core curricula for learners were introduced, based on the national standards for literacy, language and numeracy, and a Pre-Entry Curriculum Framework was designed for people with learning difficulties and disabilities, who are unable to access the national curricula. Guidance on how adults with learning difficulties and disabilities can be involved in all levels of literacy, language and numeracy learning was also published.

Many teaching and learning materials were commissioned to link to the national standards and support the core curricula. They include paper-based and web-based materials, as well as a wide range of e-learning opportunities. ICT has proved to be not only a motivator for adults to become involved in literacy, language and numeracy activities but also a lively and imaginative way for people to learn. Further curriculum development has addressed literacy, language and numeracy in the contexts of employment, community learning and vocational training, with accompanying assessment materials and resources.

Qualifications and assessment

A progressive framework of qualifications has been established, with national standards of achievement, to enable individuals to progress in their learning, and to measure progress towards the national targets. A set of national tests were developed by the Qualifications and Curriculum Authority to accompany the framework.

Inspection and quality assurance

Government produced guidance on raising standards, linked to the Common Inspection Framework for Further Education. This looked at different contexts in which the *Skills for Life* strategy would be delivered, including in FE colleges, Adult and Community Learning, Family learning, and Offender learning.

Numeracy

In England, DIUS is developing (2008) a *Numeracy for Employability Plan* which aims to reach the targets set in *World Class Skills*, that is to have, by 2020, 95 per cent of the working age population of England at or above Entry Level 3 in numeracy. There is general recognition that this target is much more challenging than those for literacy and ESOL, and that without a specific focus on numeracy, it is unlikely to be met. The strategy is likely to address several issues; the need for separate reporting of numeracy activity (until now it has often been difficult to distinguish numeracy programmes from literacy or ESOL ones, in the data produced by providers), raising demand among learners, expanding the teaching workforce, and raising the quality of provision.

In 2005 Learning Connections Scotland acted to increase the emphasis of numeracy within its Adult Literacies work. Recent projects have focussed on the use of ICT in numeracy and on numeracy for healthcare workers.

A community development model of literacy

In Scotland a more community-based approach to basic skills has been adopted, with a strong focus on personal development and community capacity building. The Adult Literacies in Scotland Project supports local authorities, voluntary organisations and FE colleges who use community education approaches and are primary deliverers of adult literacy.

The Osler Working Group Report 'Communities: Change through Learning' (1999) outlines a vision for Scotland as a democratic and socially just society that enables all of its citizens to develop their potential to the full and to have the capacity, individually and collectively, to meet the challenge of change.

The Osler Working Group believes that community education approaches have a powerful relevance to the Government's current policy agenda on social inclusion, lifelong learning, and active citizenship. They propose a radical shift where community education becomes a major contributor to building the vision outlined above. In order to achieve this, there needs to be a focus on community education's particular ways of working to develop skills, knowledge and capacity in community contexts and on three main purposes:

■ investing in community learning;
■ building community capacity;
■ promoting personal development.

The Osler Report sees literacy as embedded in personal development through community education approaches which combine:

■ Courses and projects;
■ Research;
■ Enhancing networks of support;
■ Creating access to/investing in resources;
■ Advice to external agencies;
■ Courses and projects provide adult learning opportunities for individuals and groups who have identified their own literacy learning needs through a guidance process. Courses and projects may be short or long term.

Such courses and projects should be underpinned by indirect support for literacy learning. As noted above, adults with limited literacy capabilities experience a mutually reinforcing cycle of limited demands and limited opportunities. When surveyed, the majority describe themselves as 'satisfied' with their literacy skills in their everyday lives.

Carrying out research, enhancing networks of support, creating access to/investing in resources, and giving advice to external agencies can all function as forms of indirect support for literacy learning. They can address the stigma that is, at present, attached to adult literacy learning. They can break into and ameliorate the effects of the damaging cycle that prevents the most excluded adults from developing their literacies.

■ **Research** increases our understanding of the literacies encountered and created by excluded groups and should inform the work of programme planners.
■ **Enhancing networks** of support enables excluded people to complete literacy tasks with the help of local individuals and groups where they choose to do so.
■ **Investing in and creating access to literacy resources** counters exclusion and equalises opportunities for individuals and community groups.
■ **Advice to external agencies** enables them to address the ways their literacies exclude groups and individuals whose literacies are different.

The strong correlation between limited literacy capabilities and poverty, ill health, unemployment and poor housing points to the contribution learning can make as a resource for countering inequalities and as a resource for developing the knowledge, skills and understanding to challenge and change inequalities. Analysis of the 1970 Cohort study has revealed, in both Scotland and England the association between economic and social disadvantage and low literacy, and their transmission across generations. Envisaging a full range of community education approaches to adult literacy learning is an important step in realising community education's potential as an agent for change.

The Osler Report recommends that local authorities be required to produce a community learning plan. Councils are to consult with voluntary organisations, FE colleges, adult guidance networks etc. in developing their plan and to involve learners and communities as a starting point in the planning process, rather than just as end users. Table 9 illustrates nine examples of adult literacy work, using the current policy fields and the three community education functions proposed in the Osler Report:

Table 9 Osler Models of Literacy

	Lifelong Learning	Social Inclusion	Active Citizenship
Promoting Personal Development	running an awareness-raising session for first line staff/guidance workers on the nature of adult's literacies and their learning need	offering targeted short courses to address the immediate needs of learners whose current life experiences preclude a longer commitment to learning	working on critical literacy approaches to reading and writing policy documents, with excluded groups involved in national or local decision making and consultation
Building Community Capacity	collaborating with other community education providers to offer a literacy element in courses designed to meet a specific community group's needs	developing a community literacy project to produce positive images and texts to counter external negative representations of the area	developing a community literacy project to produce positive images and texts to counter external negative representations of the area
Investing in Community Learning	initiating an outreach course to investigate local literacies with new learners and counter negative perceptions of 'popular' literacies	working with health workers to improve communication between themselves and patients by assessing the readability and bias in their information and advice	working with health workers to improve communication between themselves and patients by assessing the readability and bias in their information and advice

Commentary

The UK approach (and especially the English approach) since 2000 has been to invest very heavily in improving *Skills for Life* with a strong national programme, supported by national research, promotion, staff training, and a body of national materials, standards for teachers and learners, and qualifications. All these have been reinforced by a guarantee of free tuition and prioritising funding. However, a number of issues remain:

■ the UK (and especially the English) approach tends to privilege cognitive and functional notions of literacy over the social practice and transformative models which have been developed in some countries, and it is also prone to stigmatise learners through "deficit models" of literacy;

91 Macrae (1999)

■ tackling basic skills requires long term, and large scale, Government investment – these skills take time to develop, and it may be difficult to maintain political commitment;

■ target driven policies tend to privilege those with relatively minor difficulties and those who are more easily accessed. This has to some extent, happened, with a high proportion of measured achievements coming from people under 19.

■ A similar issue arises with ESOL needs, where recent immigrants from EU countries (who have entered in very large numbers since the EU expanded its frontiers in 2004) have been more keen to take up opportunities than long standing immigrants with poor English. There is also fear that the resources required to meet this particular need have also diverted resources from *Skills for Life* provision for British born people;

■ The focus on the economic impact of poor literacy diverts attention from older people, who may have severe problems, but have no intention of returning to the labour market;

■ A strong focus on one curriculum area has the effect of diverting resources from other groups. The focus on basic skills in England has led to a reduced supply of more general adult education, some of which has traditionally provided non-threatening entry routes to basic skills programmes;

■ The most disadvantaged people, socially and economically, are those with the lowest skill levels, but these remain the least likely to be aware of opportunities, or to perceive the benefits of taking part;

■ The need to measure individual performance, and the achievement of policy objectives, has imposed formal assessment on some people who are reluctant to become involved because of very negative experiences of testing at school;

■ The rapid expansion of a programme of this kind puts strains on the supply of teachers, especially in a field of education which is of low status, and which has traditionally depended heavily on part-time casually employed staff and volunteers. This has particularly affected ESOL teaching and learners with learning difficulties or disabilities;

■ Numeracy remains a problem area. The relationship between functional literacy and mathematics is unclear, and teachers and students in general share a fear of numbers which make it difficult to reach those with real needs. However, numeracy is increasingly seen as important, particularly for economic prosperity.

4.3 Examples of effective practice and innovative programmes

A national survey

The *Skills for Life* survey was commissioned by the Department for Education and Skills, and 8,730 randomly selected adults were interviewed in two overlapping samples. The first interview included assessments for literacy and numeracy; the second interview included two ICT tests.

The research was reported at length. Key findings included:

■ Around one in six respondents (16 per cent, or 5.2 million 16-65 year olds) were classified as having skills below Level 1 in the national qualification framework. These skills levels were associated with socio-economic deprivation.

- Adults in the highest social classes were four times more likely than those in social class five households to reach Level 2 or above in the literacy test.
- Language was a barrier to those whose first language was not English (7 per cent of the total) – only one in four achieved Level 2, but those whose first language was not English but who claimed to have 'very good' spoken English performed to a similar standard as those with English as a first language. Among those from ethnic minorities speaking English as their first language, the only group performing below the general population were of Black Caribbean origin.
- Good literacy and numeracy skills tended to be associated with good wages, although the connection was stronger for numeracy.
- Very few adults regarded their reading, writing or maths skills as below average, even among those with the lowest level of performance. Only a tiny proportion (two per cent) felt that weak skills had hindered their job prospects or led to mistakes at work.
- The majority of respondents at each level of literacy claimed to read every day, with the exception of those at Entry Level 1. One in four of these respondents said they never read, but even among this group, four in ten read every day. The frequency of writing was more closely associated with literacy level. Only one in five of those with Entry 1 or lower level literacy, and only one in three of those with Entry Level 2 literacy wrote every day.
- Nearly all parents of children aged 5–16 said they helped their children with reading (95 per cent), writing (89 per cent) or maths (87 per cent). Those with lower levels of literacy and/or numeracy were less likely to help, and were less confident when they did, but still the majority tried to help (63 per cent of those with Entry Level 2 or lower level literacy helped with their children's reading).
- Twelve per cent of respondents said they have received training (outside school) in reading, writing or speaking English. This rises to 37 per cent for those whose first language is not English. One third said they had learnt 'a great deal' and another 44 per cent said they had learned 'a fair amount' from this training.
- Many of the respondents had a relatively high level of awareness of ICT applications and terminology, but a good level of awareness was not always accompanied by good practical skills. Fifteen per cent had never used a computer and slightly fewer than half (47 per cent) achieved Level 1 or above in the practical assessment. Those who performed better were likely to use a computer most days, whether at home or work, use a computer for a variety of applications and were confident in their abilities.
- Most people accurately predicted their ICT skills, whereas many adults over-estimated their levels of literacy and numeracy.

Voluntary and community sector

A number of projects have sought to develop *Skills for Life* by building capacity in community and voluntary agencies whose primary purpose is not to offer literacy, language or numeracy provision. Embedding *Skills for Life* in their mainstream work has made it possible to reach clients who are included in the government's target groups. This has involved organisations for homeless people; those under the supervision of probation services; people experiencing mental ill-health or organisations which work in neighbourhoods experiencing particular disadvantages. The government recognised that without the contributions of voluntary organisations, its ambitions for reaching particular target groups, improvement and achievement would not be met.

Embedded approaches
A partnership with Ukonline and Learndirect delivered awareness raising and training to their staff on integrating literacy, language and numeracy in their centres, which exist to provide advice and tuition, especially in the use of ICTs. NIACE staff worked on the development of conceptual frameworks as well as to identify effective and interesting practices. NRDC, and others, have researched embedded and non-embedded approaches to delivery in Further Education colleges. The results of such research have been published, discussed and debated in a wide range of conferences, seminars and staff development events.

Family learning
Family learning, family literacy and family numeracy have been increasingly acknowledged as important planks of the government's adult learning strategy, often linked to Sure Start Centres. A national evaluation carried out by NIACE found that these programmes had contributed greatly to parents' and carers' own literacy, language and numeracy by helping them to help their children.

Dyslexia and learning difficulties and disabilities
In partnership with the former Learning and Skills Development Agency (LSDA, now the Learning and Skills Network) NIACE identified common and effective approaches to dealing with dyslexia and published a *Framework for Understanding Dyslexia*. It also led a large consortium which developed *Learning for Living* programmes for literacy, language and numeracy for people with learning difficulties and disabilities,.

The Maths4life project
This research and development project (hosted by the National Centre for Excellence in Teaching Mathematics www.ncetm.org.uk) supports adults who are learning mathematics at and below Level 2, with a particular emphasis on work at Entry Level and Level 1. It has produced research papers, resources to support collaborative professional development for teachers, and materials for learners. It emphasises the benefits to learners of working collaboratively, learning actively, exploring cognitive conflicts, and making connections among different areas of mathematics. Similar approaches, inspired by this project, are being supported in Northern Ireland.

Embedded Skills for Life in the health sector
The National Health Service is one of the largest employers in the world (with 1.5 million staff, and a total annual expenditure on training of over £5 billion). However, low levels of literacy, language and numeracy limit employment choices for non-clinical staff, and lead to risk to patients (e.g. in reading instructions, dosages, equipment manuals and health and safety guidance). In all age groups, workers in health and social care are less likely to have

level 2 skills in literacy and numeracy. This rises to 65 per cent of workers lacking literacy and 75 per cent lacking numeracy at this level among staff over 45 (who form a large proportion of the total workforce). The Department for Innovation, Universities and Skills is working jointly with the Department of Health to develop strategies and support structures for embedding *Skills for Life* provision in the operation of the health service.

English for Speakers of Other Languages (ESOL)

An exploration of formative assessment is also being undertaken, which will examine the training needs of new migrants, including asylum seekers and refugees, especially in relation to teaching and learning ESOL. A recent independent national inquiry, initiated and led by NIACE (2006), has stimulated policy and practice debate and discussion in Government as well as in the field.

4.4 How policies and programmes focus on gender, and other target groups

Gender has not been identified as a particular priority for literacy provision, although women form a core of most of the disadvantaged groups which are targeted. In practice, women dominate provision in several of the key development areas, especially family literacy. The NIACE review of ESOL found that women migrants suffer particular disadvantages. This affects both those who come as spouses to the UK and cannot get tuition on arrival and other women who have been here for some time, especially from Bangladeshi and Pakistani communities.

4.5 Policies and programmes aimed at building literate environments

The UK – like most industrialised countries – assumes a literate environment, which tends to exclude the minority with few or poor basic skills. Furthermore, as a society, the UK has developed highly specialised kinds of communication which tend to exclude people, not because they cannot read, but because the content of much writing seems detached from everyday experience for people with low literacy levels.

Two areas where this is particularly notable are health and finance. In both cases, the decisions which individuals have to make are increasingly complex, making heavy demands on the ability to interpret written and oral information. Since low levels of literacy are also associated with low levels of income and poorer health, this group tend to suffer multiple disadvantages.

Efforts to develop health and financial literacies aim to address this challenge by not only encouraging individuals to develop their skills but also to change the communication/literacy and numeracy behaviours of those who are responsible for communicating with the public. The simplification of language in public information documents has been a theme of public policy for some years, and real progress has been made, but many issues like pensions and medical treatments remain inherently complex, and are becoming more so.

The UK has a very well developed range of public libraries, which provide reference and lending facilities, information about learning opportunities (including literacy, language and numeracy services). Many also provide Internet access, and online learning facilities, sometimes incorporating *Ukonline* and *Learndirect* Centres.

The Government finances a national network of 6,000 local *Ukonline* centres where the general public can have free access to the internet, and support in using it. The *Learndirect* centres provide access in community locations (in sports clubs, leisure and community centres, churches, libraries, on university campuses and railway stations), to online adult education programmes and associated support, including some or all of: free internet access, crèches, cafés, parking, lending libraries, games rooms, and desktop publishing facilities.

5 Expectations of CONFINTEA VI and future perspectives for ALE

5.1 What the UK expects from CONFINTEA VI

Progress since CONFINTEA V

CONFINTEA set an ambitious agenda for development. On some of the issues the UK has made more progress than on others. We believe that any proposals for a new agenda from CONFINTEA VI should take full account of the progress to date on the Hamburg Declaration. We also believe that CONFINTEA VI might usefully try to focus more clearly on a more limited and deliverable agenda, and that the sheer range and scale of the Hamburg aspirations may have made it more difficult to monitor progress and ensure achievement.

In this context the UK has, as enjoined in the Hamburg Declaration, very substantially increased public expenditure on adult learning. It has, however, focused its educational expenditure strongly on particular kinds of learning in the belief that the main tool for achieving both economic and social objectives, is ensuring that all adults have access to productive and rewarding employment, and that in a global economy, the UK's long term economic future lies in highly skilled work. Many of the broader objectives identified in the Declaration are achieved through Government Departments like Health and the Home Office, or by encouraging provision by the private and third sectors.

In relation to the specific items on the Hamburg Declaration the UK has made substantial progress on:

- **Women's integration and empowerment** – overall women represent a majority of participants in post school learning and attain more too. There remain issues about women being disproportionately concentrated in particular subjects, and about participation by women from some minority ethnic groups.
- **Diversity and equality** – there has been progress, with legislation on disability, gender and age driving a broadening of access and participation in most adult learning, although there are still some issues to reaching the most marginalised groups.
- **Transformation of the economy** – this has been a major focus of UK policy development, and active labour market policies have resulted in very high labour market participation rates. However, concern remains about the large body of people with low skills, who are employed but at risk in the event of industrial change. Recent initiatives aim to overcome this with a focus on linking skills and employment to ensure sustainability of approach.
- **Access to information** – access to information technologies has spread very widely and rapidly, and public access sites and projects have provided both access and training for

many who do not have access in their homes or workplaces. However, there remains a substantial minority of people who either lack the skills or choose not to make use of ICTs. Progress has been more modest on:

■ **Culture of peace and education for citizenship and democracy** – although citizenship and social cohesion is a major strand of Government policy, this has tended to focus on the response to political extremism, rather than on the broader questions of citizenship education.

■ **Health education** – much has been achieved in this field through the Department of Health with specific campaigns and initiatives (notably in relation to smoking, where there has been a major shift in public attitudes), and more recently through active labour market policies to help people with illness and disabilities to return to the workforce. Broader health education does not feature large in the broader adult education world. However there are specific initiatives with FE colleges that DIUS has recently been working with the Department of Health to ensure closer alignment with health education.

■ **Environmental sustainability** – there has been much activity in the third sector on this issue. In the public sector this features in the way Further Education college buildings are being built, the work of a number of Sector Skills Councils and on plans to have a cross-sectoral approach to environmental skills issues.

■ **The ageing population** – Government has responded to the ageing population with a coordinated cross-Departmental strategy. However, this has not, to date, made a major impact on adult education, and one of the unintended consequences of the policy to focus public resources on employment related learning has been to reduce the number of older people participating in learning (although some of the shortfall has been taken up by a growing third sector)

The UK believes that all these objectives remain important, but that some will be better achieved through a mixture of public, private and third sector activity, and that Government intervention will sometimes come best from Government Departments with a direct concern with the specific topic.

Objectives for the future
The UK's experience since CONFINTEA V suggests that there are two major issues which adult education will have to address over the next decade.

Education for the whole person
Adult learning is often seen as the servant of particular economic, social or cultural objectives, and public expenditure on it is justified in those terms. As a result, public policy tends to treat education for individual health, citizenship and employment as if they were quite distinct. Yet individuals are not different people when at home, in their communities, or at work, and their learning "spills over" between the domains. As the tools become available to monitor and manage the performance of educational systems more precisely, there is a real risk that Governments will focus on very specific policy objectives in one domain, at the expense of the broader education of whole people. The achievements in one domain may be

clear and measurable, while the loss in other (no less important) domains less evident. Governments should be encouraged to develop models of learning which integrate the individual, social and economic dimensions of peoples' lives, reflect the complex intermixing of formal, non-formal and informal learning in each individuals' learning career, and embrace all four of the domains of learning identified in the Delors report (to know, to do, to live together and to be).

Establishing a clear contract between the individual, employer and the state

In changing and increasingly mobile societies, learning should be seen as a right across the whole lifecourse, not simply something for young people, or for those in the workforce. However, since resources are necessarily limited, such a right needs to be set in the context of the (formal or informal) "contract" between individual, state and employer over rights and responsibilities, and entitlement to support (including funding). Such a contract should recognise that opportunities to learn (formal, informal and non-formal) will always be made by a combination of public, private and third sector organisations). It would also recognise the importance of learning which contributes social benefits like the transmission of knowledge and culture between generations, and social cohesion.

At its most basic we would suggest that the state has a responsibility to provide every individual with the levels of literacy, numeracy and familiarity with current information and communication technologies required to play a full part as a citizen, as a parent/grandparent and worker. This should be available to adults of all ages (including those who have retired from the workforce), regardless of gender, ethnic origin, employment status or social class.

The state also has some responsibility to ensure that the underlying institutional framework to support adult learning remains relatively stable over time, to enable individuals to plan and manage learning careers across their lifespan, and organisations and teachers to work without undue administrative pressures or organisational turbulence.

Issues for UNESCO

In addition to the two major issues identified above, UNESCO has a clear and special interest in international dimensions of adult learning. In an increasingly mobile and globalised world there are a number of areas where increasing globalisation makes international collaboration increasingly important. UNESCO should take particular interest in the following issues:

- **Learner engagement**: to support and share good practice on the involvement of learners in the design, management and quality assurance of adult learning. This will improve the quality and relevance of learning opportunities.
- **Mobility**: mechanisms to enable individuals to move as freely as possible across national frontiers, with opportunities to acquire the language, learn about the culture, and have their qualifications recognised so that they can play a full part as workers and citizens of the host country. This will help minimise the waste of talent and restrictions on opportunity for individuals.
- **Access to resources**: to develop processes and structures for the sharing and dissemination of learning resources across national and regional frontiers, to maximise opportunities to

learn while respecting national cultural and political distinctiveness. Issues involve the development of law on intellectual property and copyright, on open access learning materials, and access to technologies for learning (recognising the complex and varying combinations of technology available in different countries, including technologies like social networking which have educational potential, despite being designed for different purposes). This will provide a wider range of opportunities to learners worldwide without imposing culturally inappropriate models or approaches.

- **Quality**: to establish systems and instruments for quality assurance in ALE which reflect the diversity of learners and the complexity of learning needs, and the need to monitor and improve performance without placing an unmanageable administrative burden on providers. This will help improve the quality and relevance of learning, to the benefit of learners, economies and societies.
- **Comparative research**: to support the development of research to explore ways of promoting, supporting and developing adult learning, and to develop methodologies for mutual learning and transfer. This will enable countries to learn effectively from each others' experience.

5.2 Issues to be addressed in adult education in the UK

The following issues are priorities for the UK over the next decade:

- Improve the skills of the population throughout their working lives to create a workforce capable of sustaining economic competitiveness, and enable individuals to thrive in the knowledge economy.
- Build social and community cohesion through improved social justice, civic participation and economic opportunity by raising aspirations and broadening participation, progression and achievement in learning and skills.
- Strengthen the capacity, quality and reputation of the Further and Higher Education systems and institutions to support national economic and social needs.

To achieve this we need to ensure

- that better education, research and innovation outputs translate into better economic and social outcomes
- that employers and learners are convinced that it is worth investing more of their time, money and energy in education, training and skills on the scale needed to meet the Government's objectives
- sufficient institutional stability to ensure that the delivery partners (Colleges and Universities, as well as publicly funded work based learning agencies and Local Authorities) are not distracted from delivering the ongoing service through uncertainty over the future organisational shape of the sector, or the scale of change

Particular issues to be addressed include

■ Creating a demand-led education system across the whole of adult learning
■ Supporting individuals to develop the skills to find, retain and progress in work
■ Raising the skills levels of those with lowest qualifications, who are vulnerable in an increasingly high skilled economy.
■ Strengthen the student voice in education policy
■ Widen participation in higher education
■ Develop appropriate structures to support a healthy range of informal learning
■ Develop a universal careers guidance service to assist all individuals to manage their careers, in and outside of paid work

Annex 1
Major programmes

Table 1

Programme name	a) Provider			b) Area of learning			Target groups	Funding source
	Public/State	CSO/NGO	Private	General competencies	Technical skills	Knowledge generation, innovation		
Train to Gain	x		x	x	x	x	Employer needs	Government
Skills for Life	x	x	x	x			Low basic skills	Government
Apprenticeships	x		x	x	X			Government
Personal and Community Development Learning	x	x	x	x		x	General adults	Government
Informal learning		x	x	x		x	General adults	Individuals
Higher Education degree programmes	x			x	x	x	Qualified young people and adults	Government
Higher Education continuing education	x			x	x	x	General adults	Individuals
Higher education continuing professional development	x				x	x	Employees	Employers/individuals
Employer programmes			x	x	x	x	Employees	Employers
New Deal	x	x	x	x	x		Unemployed	Government
Learndirect	x				x		General adults	Government

Annex 2
Timeline of major policy events 1997–2008

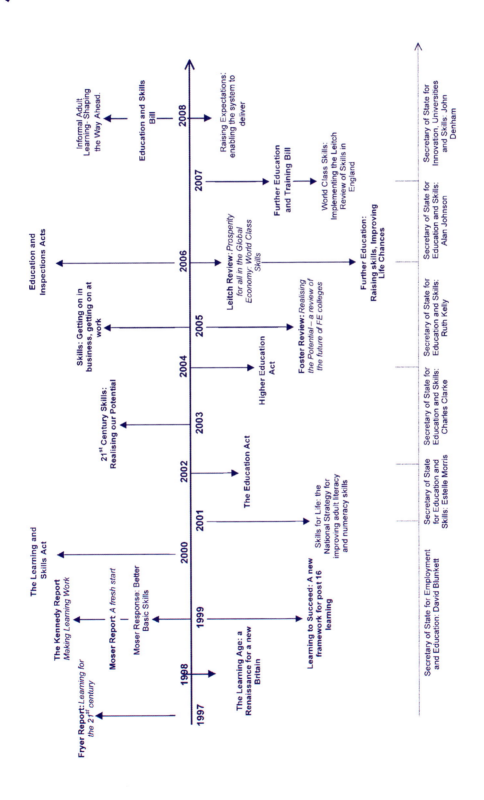

Annex 3
Glossary of terms

Adult and Community Learning	One of a series of terms used to describe non-accredited non-formal adult education programmes. Other terms include "Non-Schedule 2" (from a legal definition), "Safeguarded Learning" (because of a Government guarantee to protect/safeguard the budget for this work); Personal and Community Development Learning (to try to reflect some of its purposes. The repeated renaming reflects the uncertainty among policymakers about its importance.
Awarding bodies	Agencies (public or private) which are recognised to provide academic or vocational qualifications – setting curricula and managing assessment.
Apprenticeships	Apprenticeships are nationally designed training programmes for those who have already left full time education or are already in employment. They provide a combination of on and off-the-job training whilst being paid. There are two levels of Apprenticeships: the Apprenticeship and the Advanced Apprenticeship which typically take between one and three years to complete.
Continuing Professional Development (CPD):	A range of short and long training programmes, sometimes with the option of formal accreditation, which foster the development of employment-related knowledge, skills and understanding.
DIUS	Department of Innovation, Universities and Skills. The English Department responsible for Further, Higher, Adult and Workbased learning. Formed in 2007 by splitting the former Department for Education and Skills (DfES)
ESOL:	English for Speakers of Other Languages
Foundation Degree:	A 2 year vocational higher education qualification. The development of Foundation Degrees aims to increase the number of people qualified at higher technician and associate professional level, such as legal executives, engineering technicians and personnel officers. (see 3.2.1)

Further Education: Education after compulsory schooling (i.e. after 16). Legally, the term includes all learning below higher education level. This includes academic and vocational qualification courses, "work based learning" provided by private sector training agencies, and non-accredited programmes for adults.

Further Education Colleges (FECs): FE Colleges provide academic and vocational qualifications for people over 16. Some focus mainly on people 16-19 in the final phase of secondary education, others mainly on adults, but most provide a mix of these.

Higher Education Funding Council for England (HEFCE): Distributes public money to universities and colleges for teaching and research. The council's brief is to promote high quality education and research. It also plays a role in ensuring accountability and promoting good practice. There are separate funding councils for Wales, Scotland and Northern Ireland.

IAG: Information, Advice and Guidance, the generic term used for services providing advice on education, training and career to adults

ICT: Information and communication technologies, for learning and for other purposes.

ITT: Initial Teacher Training

JANET: The "Joint Academic Network". A consortium of national bodies who jointly support high speed internet connections for educational institutions, and a range of supporting services for users and technical staff.

JISC: A national partnership of agencies which provides support to the national infrastructure for IT in Further and Higher Education, including broadband access and support to institutions and staff.

Learning and Skills Council (LSC): A "Non-Departmental Public Body" created in 2001 responsible for planning and funding education and training for people over 16 in England other than those in universities. It has a national office and nine regional offices. Its annual budget for 2006–07 is £10.4 billion.

Learndirect: A national Government funded agency which provides a network of online learning centres, and telephone and online advice and support on careers and learning to the general public. www.learndirect.co.uk

Levels: Formal qualifications in the UK are defined in terms of
"levels" in the various qualification frameworks.
Entry Levels 1–3: three levels used mainly in Skills for Life
provision, below the main Level 1 in the framework.
Level 1: ISCED Level 1. In the UK these qualifications
include GCSEs, O-Levels or equivalent at grades D–G;
National Vocational Qualification (NVQ) Level 1; Business
Training and Education Council (BTEC) First or General
Certificate; General National Vocational Qualification
(GNVQ) Foundation Level; Royal Society of Arts (RSA) and
SCOTVEC modules.
Level 2: ISCED Level 2. Five or more GCSEs, O-Levels or
equivalent at grades A–C; NVQ Level 2; BTEC First or
General Diploma; GNVQ Intermediate Level; City and
Guilds Craft; RSA diploma; and BTEC, SCOTVEC First or
General Diploma.
Level 3: ISCED Level 3. Two or more A-Levels or equivalent;
NVQ Level 3; BTEC National; Ordinary National Diploma
(OND); Ordinary National Certificate (ONC); City and
Guilds Advanced Craft.
Level 4: ISCED Level 4. First or other degree; NVQ Level 4;
Higher National Diploma (HND); Higher National
Certificate (HNC); and higher education diploma; nursing;
teaching (including further education, secondary, primary
and others).
Level 5: ISCED Level 5. Higher degree; Doctor of Philosophy
(Ph.D.); and NVQ Level 5.

Lifelong Learning UK: The Sector Skills Council which represents employers in
the development of qualifications for Further Education
teaching staff.

NRDC: The National Research and Development Centre for Adult
Literacy and Numeracy – studies the teaching of literacy and
numeracy (see Annex 3);

OCNs: Open College Networks (see 2.1.3) are local/regional
consortia of education providers which negotiate
equivalences between locally designed adult programmes,
and award credit to students on such accredited
programmes.

Public Service Agreements: PSAs define the Government's high-level priorities. They
set out the specific improvements that the Government
wants to achieve across all Departments, and the
performance indicators which will be used to measure

progress. Each PSA is underpinned by a Delivery Agreement which outlines how improvements will be achieved, and which Department of Agency will be accountable for delivery.

Qualifications and Credit Framework:

A national framework being developed by the QCA in consultation with other agencies. It is intended to recognise a wide range of learning achievements that are relevant to their particular occupation and/or signify competence in a particular field.

Qualified Teacher Status (QTS):

The formal requirement to teach in schools (includes a formal qualification and supervised teaching experience). A similar requirement has been introduced recently to teachers in Further Education. There is now an expectation that teachers in higher education undertake training, but there is no formal national requirement of the same kind as QTS..

Quality Assurance Agency for Higher Education (QAA):

Safeguards and helps to improve the academic standards and quality of higher education in the UK.

Quality Improvement Agency:

QIA is a Government agency set up in 2005 to support Further Education providers to improve performance and implement the Government's reforms for learning and skills. From June 2008, the QIA will be transferring to a new sector-owned improvement body together with the Centre for Excellence in Leadership.

OFFA:

The Office for Fair Access in Education is the Regulator for higher education whose remit is to ensure that higher education institutions are actively promoting fair and wider access through their admissions processes and policies and schemes of financial support.

Ofsted:

The Office for Standards in Education. The non-ministerial government department with responsibility for the inspection of all schools and all adult education outside higher education.

QCF:

National Qualifications and Credit Framework (see 2.1.4)

RARPA:

Recognising and Recording Progress and Achievement is a process developed by NIACE and the LSC to provide a measure for non-accredited adult education to compare with the formal qualification measures used in the rest of Further Education.

SSDA:

Sector Skills Development Agency. National organisation to

support the Sector Skills Councils with research and development work. Functions transferred in 2008 to UKCES

SSCs: The 25 Sector Skills Councils are employer led bodies which represent employers in each of the 25 occupational sectors for the economy. Together they cover over 85 per cent of the UK workforce and operate across the whole of the UK

Sure Start: A major Government programme to deliver the best start in life for every child, by linking early years education, childcare, health and family support. It focuses particularly on disadvantaged communities, and includes a significant element of family and parent education, including basic skills programmes.
www.surestart.gov.uk/

Train to Gain: A Government service designed to help business of all types and sizes get the training they need to succeed. It is managed by the Learning and Skills Council (LSC) across England. It uses experienced Skills Brokers who work closely with individual businesses to identify the skills the particular business needs, pinpoint the right training, agree a tailored training package, find available funding and review progress.

UKCES The UK Commission for Employment and Skills. An employer led body, created in 2008 to lead the development of the UK employment skills base. Incorporates the former Sector Skills Development Agency (SSDA)

UKOnline: A Government initiative which provides 6,000 local centres in a wide range of locations. Each Centre provides free public access to the Internet and advice and support in using it.

Union Learning Fund: A government initiative launched 1998 to encourage a range of vocational and non-vocational education projects rooted in the workplace.

Union Learning Representatives: Members of recognised Trades Union appointed by their Union to promote learning in the workplace, with statutory rights specified in the Employment Act 2002.

Annex 4
Major research centres and programmes

The Foresight Unit
The Foresight Unit of the Office of the Government Chief Scientist, is funded to study the implications of leading edge research and development for social and economic policy and public services. It seeks to examine likely technological, scientific and sociological developments over future decades. In 2007, the Unit began a major 2 year study of "*Mental Capital and Wellbeing*", steered by academic expert groups, and with commissioned papers from experts worldwide, drawn from fields including education, neurosciences, economics, information technology, sociology, and medicine. The project aims to identify long term trends and expectations in issues including: learning capacity; enhancement and the development and decline of cognitive performance across the lifecourse; mental health; intervention strategies to improve performance or defer deterioration; the economic impact of wellbeing and learning; and institutional structures to support learning . The study will report in 2009.

The Centre for Research on the Wider Benefits of Learning
The Centre is funded by Government at the Institute of Education, London University, to study the non-economic benefits of education, using, inter alia, the longitudinal cohort studies. Its reports include studies of:
■ the role of adult education in overcoming the impact of poor schooling
■ the impact of adult education on adult attitudes on social cohesion and political activity, and attitudes to social issues like race
■ the impact of adult education on health, crime reduction and social capital

www.learningbenefits.net

The Centre for the Economics of Education
The Centre is funded by Government at the London School of Economics, to undertake systematic and innovative interdisciplinary research in the economics of education. It has carried out studies of:
■ The economic impact of low literacy and numeracy skills across the lifecourse
■ The impact of the introduction of student fees on participation in higher education
■ The impact of growing international student mobility
■ The labour market value of education, qualifications, and skills, including "soft skills"

- Development of human capital across the lifecourse
- The labour market value of basic skills

cee.lse.ac.uk

The Centre for Longitudinal Studies

The centre is funded by ESRC at the Institute of Education to house three major longitudinal research studies, of people born in 1958, 1970 and 2000. These cohorts are surveyed repeatedly across the lifecourse, allowing sophisticated analysis of a range of social and economic factors. The Centre also has access to the first such cohort survey, of people born in 1946, which is also used in some of its research.

A wide range of social and economic research has been based on this data, and especially on the education and health issues. In education notable work has been done on:

- the economic returns to education over a lifetime
- access to higher education
- the non-economic benefits of participation in post compulsory education
- the role of personal agency in entry to employment.

www.cls.ioe.ac.uk

The Centre for Research in Lifelong Learning

CRLL was created in 1999 as a joint initiative between Glasgow Caledonian University and the University of Stirling to carry out research and related activities to inform policy and provision in the field of lifelong learning in the post-compulsory sector in Scotland and beyond. It was initially funded by a Research Development Grant from the Scottish Higher Education Funding Council for its first three years, but is now self-funding. The Centre provides an opportunity for informed debate in key areas through Scottish Forum for Lifelong Learning, seminars and a biennial international conference. It publishes briefing papers related to its research projects and substantial research reports, details of which can be found its site.

crll.gcal.ac.uk

The Centre for Research and Development in adult and lifelong learning

CRADALL is based at the University of Glasgow. Its focus is on social purpose and community based learning to support adult education and lifelong learning in making a real difference to social justice, social inclusion and poverty reduction. It is self-sustaining through its funded research projects. It publishes a poverty reduction newsletter and organises regular seminars and other events.

www.gla.ac.uk/centres/cradall/index.shtml

PASCAL Observatory

The Pascal International Observatory was created in 2002 to carry out research into the fields of place management, social capital and lifelong learning. It grew out of earlier OECD work on learning regions and regional development. And was initially based on three founding member regions, Kent in England, Victoria in Australia, and Scotland. It is a significant international NGO based in Europe at the University of Glasgow and in Australia at RMIT University. It has a subscription service for regions and universities, and works mainly through a panel of highly experienced associates in areas of public governance, regional development, higher education and lifelong learning.

www.obs-pascal.com

National Research and Development Centre for Adult Literacy and Numeracy

The NRDC is funded by Government to provide the research and development necessary to underpin Government's basic skills strategy Skills for Life . It aims to provide underpinning evidence and practical guidance to teacher educators and other professionals. Its current programme has 5 themes:
- economic development and social inclusion
- participation, motivation and engagement
- effective teaching and learning
- professional development of teachers of basic skills
- infrastructure

www.nrdc.org.uk

Evidence for Policy and Practice Information and Coordinating Centre (EPPI)

The EPPI Centre is a unit of the Institute of Education, London University, funded by the ESRC to undertake systematic reviews of research evidence on areas of social policy interest, and to develop research methodology. To date its reviews of issues in post compulsory education include work on:
- participation in post-compulsory education
- participation by ethnic minority groups
- language learning
- workbased learning

eppi.ioe.ac.uk/cms/

The Teaching and Learning Research Programme (TLRP)

The TLRP is funded from 2000 to 2009 by the UK Economic and Social Research Council to study learning and its outcomes at all stages of the lifecourse, drawing on a wide range of academic disciplines. It has funded over a hundred research activities, including 34 projects in post school education,[92] ranging in length from 6 months to five years. Particular themes have included closer understanding of teaching and learning processes and their effectiveness; the role of social and cultural factors in promoting or constraining learning, and participation in programmes; studies of learning careers and trajectories; the nature of workplace learning, and particularly of expansive and restrictive workplace cultures. A range of studies have examined aspects of professional learning, from early careers to life history studies. A further strand of work has examined uses of technology in learning, mainly in relation to school pupils, but some including studies of particular aspects of professional learning, and others, like the use of computer animation in sign language for the deaf, with applications to older people.

Methods have included longitudinal studies of cohorts of learners, surveys, literature reviews, controlled trials of particular approaches, and ethnographical studies.

A particular emphasis as been placed on dissemination, enhancing policy relevance and capacity building n the research community. To assist with this, a result a great deal of material is available online via the TLRP website, and the programme has supported a wide range of seminars and events, and researchers have contributed to conferences and journals within the UK and internationally. Annex 5 lists all the TLRP projects related to post-school learning.

www.tlrp.org

Centre on Skills, Knowledge and Organisational Performance (SKOPE)

Since 1998 the ESRC has funded the Universities of Warwick, Oxford and Cardiff (the SKOPE consortium) to explore workplace learning, focusing on the relationship s between the acquisition of skills and knowledge, product market strategies and performance. The programme has produced 110 publications to date, and has now been awarded a third 5 year phase of funding. The current phase is concerned with three themes:

■ models of competitive advantage, organisational performance and managerial capabilities;
■ workforce and workplace development;
■ design and operation of the vocational education and training system, and the political economy of skill.

www.skope.ox.ac.uk

The Learning Society Programme

This multi-disciplinary programme funded 15 major projects between 1994 and 2000. It aimed to investigate:

■ the links between learning and economic success, between training and competitiveness, and between education, innovation and wealth creation?
■ the economic, political and cultural factors are preventing or facilitating the progress of the

---

92 excluding studies of children with potential applications to adults – especially in technology related learning

UK towards becoming a learning society and how can the impact of the former be minimised and the impact of the latter be maximised?

◼ the theoretical gaps in the understanding of the processes of learning and of the complex inter-relationships between employment, training and education?

◼ What can be learned from the advances being made in this area by our partners in the European Union and by the other leading industrial countries in America and the Far East?

◼ the changes should be introduced to the current systems of post-compulsory education, training and continuing education to respond to the challenges represented by a learning society?

www.ncl.ac.uk/learning.society

Annex 5
The ESRC Teaching and Learning Research Programme

Aims of the TLRP Programme

The Teaching and Learning Research Programme has six distinct aims. They relate to performing and promoting excellent educational research and ensuring that it is used to enhance learning. The aims are:

Learning

The TLRP conducts research with the potential to improve outcomes for learners in a very wide range of UK contexts across the lifecourse.

The Programme explores synergies between different research approaches and aims to build UK capacity in conducting high quality educational research.

TLRP is committed to the application of findings to policy and practice. We work to maximise the impact of our research and to present it in an accessible way.

Outcomes

TLRP studies a broad range of learning outcomes. These include both the acquisition of skill, understanding, knowledge and qualifications and the development of attitudes, values and identities relevant to a learning society.

Lifecourse

TLRP supports research projects on many ages and stages in education, training and lifelong learning. The Programme is concerned with patterns of success and difference, inclusion and exclusion through the lifecourse.

Enrichment

The TLRP is committed to engaging users in its work. It works in all disciplines and sectors of education and uses a wide range of appropriate methodology. We cooperate with other researchers within and beyond the UK whenever it is appropriate.

Expertise

TLRP works to enhance capacity for all forms of research on teaching and learning, and for research-informed policy and practice.

Improvement

The TLRP works to develop the UK knowledge base on teaching and learning and to make sure that the knowledge it develops is applied in practice and policy.

TLRP Projects in post-school learning

This table lists the research projects in aspects of lifelong learning funded by the UK Economic and Social Research Council's programme since its launch in 2000. It excludes projects specifically aimed at school age children, and some technology related projects which explore applications of technology to learning in schools which might have some implications or potential for adults.

Full details of all projects can be found on the Programme Website at www.tlrp.org

Most of the projects have their own websites with fuller information.

Further and Post 16 Education	Study of	Dates
Transforming Learning Cultures in Further Education	Four year longitudinal study of the effect of different learning cultures in 16 further education colleges.	2001–05
Learning in Community-based Further Education	Study of learning cultures in community based further education	2003–05
Literacies for Learning in Further Education	Study of impact of diverse formal and informal "literacies" on students in further education	2003–06
Policy, Learning and Inclusion in the Learning and Skills Sector	Impact of national policy on teaching, learning and assessment in Further Education	2003–06
Bilingual Literacies for Learning in Further Education	Informal and formal literacies in a bilingual context	2005–07 (Welsh project)
Learning and working in Further Education in Wales	Ethnographic study of the impact on learning of student-teacher interaction in a wider social context	2004–07

Higher Education	Study of	Dates
The Effectiveness of Problem Based Learning in Promoting Evidence Based Practice	Cochrane review of literature on the effectiveness of problem based medical ducation, and a randomised controlled trial in nurse education	2002–03

Higher Education	Study of	Dates
Enhancing Teaching-Learning Environments in Undergraduate Courses	Ways of encouraging high quality undergraduate learning. Collaborative research in 28 course teams from three Universities to study	2001–04
What is Learned at University: The Social and Organisational Mediation of Learning	The relationship between social and organisational factors and student outcomes.	2004–07
Disabled Students' Learning in Higher Education	Impact of type of disability, subject and institution on student experience and outcomes	2004–07
Learning to Perform: Instrumentalists and Instrumental Teachers	Development of expertise in music, and applications in other fields. Four year longitudinal study of students	2004–08
The social-cultural and learning experiences of working class students in higher education	The relationship between social class, he experience of students in higher education, and their performance	2006–08
Non-participation in HE: Decision-making as an embedded social practice	Impact of "networks of intimacy" on decisions to participate in HE at various ages	2006–07
Degrees of success: The transition between VET and HE	Transitions between vocational programmes and higher education	2006–08
Learning and teaching for social diversity and difference	Teachers and students conceptions of themselves and their roles, with a diverse range of students	2006–08
Widening participation in higher education: A quantitative analysis	Analysis of HE participation by class, ethnicity, gender, maturity. Examines both entry and experience of HE, through quantitative analysis of large national datasets	2006–07
Universal Access and Dual Regimes of Further and Higher Education	Impact of the UK division between Further and Higher Education institutions on attempts to widen participation in HE	2006–08

Higher Education	Study of	Dates
Investigating Musical Performance (IMP): Comparative Studies in Advanced Musical Learning	How musicians and performers develop learning about performance in HE and in community settings	2006–08

Workplace Learning	Study of	Dates
Improving Incentives to Learning in the Workplace	Apprenticeship models of learning, and the role of tacit skills and knowledge and expansive v restrictive working cultures on workplace learning	2000–03
Early Career Learning at Work: LINEA	The learning of professionals in early careers in accountancy, nursing and engineering	2001–04
Learning as Work: Teaching and Learning Processes in the Contemporary Work Organisation	Roles of formal and informal learning, and expansive v restrictive working cultures on workplace learning	2003–08
Understanding the System: Techno-mathematical Literacies in the Workplace	Design and test programmes to develop "techno-mathematical literacies" among experienced employees, integrating mathematical, ICT and workplace specific information	2003–07
Enhancing 'Skills for Life': Adult Basic Skills and Workplace Learning	Assess the impact of workplace linked basic skills programmes on life chances and productivity	2003–07
Globalisation and Skill Formation Strategies of Multinational Companies: A Comparative Analysis	The roles of national and global skills strategies in multinational companies in seven countries	2004–06

Professional Learning	Study of	Dates
Competence-based Learning in the Early Professional Development of Teachers	Developing a research based model of early professional learning for teachers	2003–07

Professional Learning	Study of	Dates
Vicarious Learning and Teaching of Clinical Reasoning Skills	The role of "vicarious learning" – i.e. observing the learning of others – in professional education; and the role of multimedia case databases in the professional learning of speech therapists	2004–06
Learning in and for Interagency Working	Developing and testing a model for professional learning for interagency working in childcare	2004–07

Lifelong Learning	Study of	Dates
Learning Lives: Learning, Identity and Agency in the Lifecourse	The nature of learning across the lifecourse, through a longitudinal life history study of 130 adults and a survey of 1200 adults	2003–07
Older people and lifelong learning: choices and experiences	The reasons why older people (post-employment) do or do not participate in learning, and its impact on their lives	2000–02

Technology Enhanced Learning	Study of	Dates
Transforming perspectives: technology to support the teaching and learning of threshold concepts	Uses of technology to enhance learning in relation to "threshold concepts" which are transformative, integrative and troublesome	2006–07
Workplace personalised learning environments for the development of employees' technical communicative skills	Understanding of potential of PLEs in developing technical communicative skills with diverse audiences in the workplace	2006–07
Personalisation of learning: constructing an interdisciplinary research space	Ethnographic study of adult learners' use of "digital artefacts" in personalised learning	2006–07

Annex 6
Ten principles of effective adult pedagogy

The Economic and Social Research Council's national Teaching and Learning Research Programme funded over 100 research projects to examine post school learning. The programme team reviewed the findings of all these, and identified the following set of ten principles of good adult pedagogy which they believe are supported by sound research.

1. *Effective pedagogy equips learners for life in its broadest sense. Learning should aim to help individuals and groups to develop the intellectual, personal and social resources that will enable them to participate as active citizens, contribute to economic development and flourish as individuals in a diverse and changing society. This means adopting a broad conception of worthwhile learning outcomes and taking seriously issues of equity and social justice for all.*

2. *Effective pedagogy engages with valued forms of knowledge. Pedagogy should engage learners with the big ideas, key skills and processes, modes of discourse, ways of thinking and practising, attitudes and relationships, which are the most valued learning processes and outcomes in particular contexts. They need to understand what constitutes quality, standards and expertise in different settings.*

3. *Effective pedagogy recognises the importance of prior experience and learning. Pedagogy should take account of what the learner knows already in order for them, and those who support their learning, to plan their next steps. This includes building on prior learning but also taking account of the personal and cultural experiences of different groups of learners.*

4. *Effective pedagogy requires learning to be scaffolded. Teachers, trainers and all those, including peers, who support the learning of others, should provide activities, cultures and structures of intellectual, social and emotional support to help learners to move forward in their learning. The learning needs to be secure when these supports are removed.*

5. *Effective pedagogy needs assessment to be congruent with learning. Assessment should be designed and implemented with the goal of achieving maximum validity both in terms of learning outcomes and learning processes. It should help to advance learning as well as determine whether learning has occurred.*

6. *Effective pedagogy promotes the active engagement of the learner. A chief goal of learning should be the promotion of learners' independence and autonomy. This involves acquiring a repertoire of learning strategies and practices, developing positive learning dispositions, and having the will and confidence to become agents in their own learning.*

7. *Effective pedagogy fosters both individual and social processes and outcomes. Learners should be encouraged and helped to build relationships and communication with others for learning purposes, in order to assist the mutual construction of knowledge and enhance the*

achievements of individuals and groups. Consulting learners about their learning and giving them a voice is both an expectation and a right.

8. *Effective pedagogy recognises the significance of informal learning. Informal learning, such as learning out of school or away from the workplace, should be recognised as at least as significant as formal learning and should therefore be valued and appropriately utilised in formal processes.*

9. *Effective pedagogy depends on the learning of all those who support the learning of others. The need for lecturers, teachers, trainers and co-workers to learn continuously in order to develop their knowledge and skill, and adapt and develop their roles, especially through practice-based inquiry, should be recognised and supported.*

10. *Effective pedagogy demands consistent policy frameworks with support for learning as their primary focus. Organisational and system level policies need to recognise the fundamental importance of continual learning – for individual, team, organisational and system success – and be designed to create effective learning environments for all learners.*

Annex 7
Public Sector Agreements 2007

Eleven of the 30 Public Service Agreements have some implications for adult learning, directly or indirectly. These are listed below, with the performance indicators relevant to adult learning (there are other indicators, not shown here, for many of the PSAs).

PSA	Agreement	Indicators relevant to adult learning
1	Raise the productivity of the UK economy	1: Labour productivity (output per hour worked) over the economic Cycle 2: International comparisons of labour productivity (per worker, per hour worked)
2	Improve the skills of the population, on the way to ensuring a world-class skills base by 2020	1: Proportion of people of working age achieving functional literacy and numeracy skills 2: Proportion of working age adults qualified to at least full Level 2 3: Proportion of working age adults qualified to at least full Level 3 4: Proportion of apprentices who complete the full apprentice framework 5: Proportion of working age adults qualified to Level 4 and above 6: Higher Education participation rate
8	Maximise employment opportunity for all	1: An increase in the overall employment rate taking account of the economic cycle 2: A narrowing of the gap between the employment rates of the following disadvantaged groups and the overall rate: disabled people, lone parents, ethnic minorities, people aged 50 and over, those with no qualifications, those living in the most deprived local authority wards

PSA	Agreement	Indicators relevant to adult learning
10	Raise the educational achievement of all children and young people	5: Proportion of young people achieving Level 2 at age 19 6: Proportion of young people achieving Level 3 at age 19
11	Narrow the gap in educational achievement between children from low income and disadvantaged backgrounds and their peers	6: The gap between the initial participation in full time higher education rates for young people aged 18, 19 and 20 from the top three and bottom four socio-economic classes
14	Increase the number of children and young people on the path to success	1: Reduce the percentage of 16-18 year olds not in education, employment or training (NEET)
15	Address the disadvantage that individuals experience because of their gender, race, disability, age, sexual orientation, religion or belief	4: Discrimination in employment 5: Fairness of treatment by services
16	Increase the proportion of socially excluded adults in settled accommodation and employment, education or training	Indicators 5–8: Proportion of socially excluded adults in employment, education or Training: – offenders – care leavers – adults in contact with secondary mental health services – adults with moderate to severe learning disabilities
17	Tackle poverty and promote greater independence and wellbeing in later life	1: The employment rate of those aged 50–69 and difference between this and the overall employment rate 4: The proportion of people over 65 who are satisfied with their home and their neighbourhood.
21	Build more cohesive, empowered and active communities	1: The percentage of people who believe people from different backgrounds get on well together in their local area 2: The percentage of people who have meaningful interactions with people from different backgrounds

PSA	Agreement	Indicators relevant to adult learning
		3: The percentage of people who feel that they belong to their neighbourhood 4: The percentage of people who feel they can influence decisions in their Locality 5: A thriving third sector 6: The percentage of people who participate in culture or sport
30	Reduce the impact of conflict through enhanced UK and international efforts	4: More effective UK capability to prevent, manage and resolve conflict and build peace